# ARMOR BEARERS

# ARMOR BEARERS

## THE REVOLUTIONARY CHOICES OF
## SERVANT-LEADERSHIP

# GERALD WATFORD

## AMBASSADOR INTERNATIONAL
GREENVILLE, SOUTH CAROLINA & BELFAST, NORTHERN IRELAND

www.ambassador-international.com

# Armorbearers

## The Revolutionary Choices of Servant-Leadership

ISBN: 978-1-62020-299-9
eISBN: 978-1-62020-349-1

Cover design and typesetting: Hannah Nichols
E-book conversion: Anna Riebe

AMBASSADOR INTERNATIONAL
Emerald House
427 Wade Hampton Blvd.
Greenville, SC 29609, USA
www.ambassador-international.com

AMBASSADOR BOOKS
The Mount
2 Woodstock Link
Belfast, BT6 8DD, Northern Ireland, UK
www.ambassadormedia.co.uk

The colophon is a trademark of Ambassador

To My Sons

# CONTENTS

# PREFACE

MY CLASSROOMS IN SERVANT-LEADERSHIP HAVE included standing by the side of the President of the United States; lying on a deserted highway, trying to defend myself against someone who was trying to kill me; facing off against my sons in a fencing bout marking their passage into manhood; and kneeling beside a good friend in prayer as we sought earnestly for God's answers. These are just a few of the places where I have struggled to learn the lessons of servant-leadership.

There is a great need for effective leadership today. We see that need in our nation, in our churches, in our families, and even in ourselves. *Armorbearers* addresses this critical need in the world today. We can change programs, plans, and procedures, but if we don't change ourselves, we will not experience what is fully available to us as Christians. By "changing ourselves" I don't mean that the power to change comes from self-effort or our trying harder. The power to change comes from a deeper relationship with the living God, who stands ever ready to supply abundantly. Relating better to God will inevitably result in better relationships with those around us.

The choices every servant-leader must make are revolutionary, not in the sense that they are new, but in the sense that they are overlooked and discarded in favor of making much of self. Right choices must be rediscovered. The principles of servant-leadership were written down in scripture many centuries ago and they have resurfaced at various times across the sweep of human history. Our times cry out for effective leadership as much as any other time.

My desire for this book is that it will guide the way back to an understanding of what it means to truly be a servant-leader. Rediscovering the principles of servant-leadership will take place, not as a lecture, but alongside a life lived with all its ups and downs. I was introduced to servant-leadership as a young Marine stationed at the White House in Washington, DC on the staff of President Reagan. At the time, I didn't know this concept had a name, but as I watched the President and others, I knew there was something different about the way they led. This started my search for excellence in service and leadership. A passion for this subject was ignited and grows stronger each day. I invite you to join me on this journey.

Gerald Watford
December 2, 2013
Columbia, South Carolina

# INTRODUCTION

WHEREVER HUMAN GREATNESS IS FOUND, it is through the application of well-kept rules that are embraced out of a desire to make much of God. I know, this does not sound as romantic as greatness being a product of our genius. However, we are children of the living God. Our purpose is to bring glory to Him by making a positive difference in the lives of others. To live this life, we must make certain choices: choices that will leave us with the strength and humility to fulfill this purpose. To live this life, we are put on a path of pursuing greatness through developing a character forged on the anvil of self-restraint and tested through the heat of self-discipline.

Who are you? It is a simple question, yet it poses such a challenge. For some of us, the question is mysterious, because we have not truly sought the answer. For others of us, the question is challenging, because we are afraid of what we might learn. For all of us, the question is unavoidable, because it lies at the root of why we make the choices we make and live the lives we live. A clearer grasp of who we are and how we got this way will improve our interaction with our God, our circumstances, and our companions.

Often there is a distinction between who we think we are, or would like to be, and who we actually are, especially under pressure or stress. Our lives contain those excruciatingly tantalizing moments where we can see the target of a better us, only to subsequently come to the conclusion that such a target is out of reach. How do we attain what we identify as essential for significant life changes? In the following pages I will answer that question by asking you to make a series of choices. These are the choices that are essential to living the life of a servant-leader. These are the choices of the armorbearer whom you will get to know quite well.

---

## We cannot overcome what is before us if we are unsure what is inside of us.

---

First, let's look more closely at ourselves. To best see ourselves, we must look at ourselves in the middle of life's trials. Whom will we be in life's toughest moments, and is there any way to better equip ourselves to be the person we would like to be, no matter how difficult the circumstances we face?

As we see ourselves in a brighter light, there will be an obvious and almost overwhelming urge to fix ourselves. Many of us already live with a passion for fixing others. But—and this is a key point to remember—we cannot fix ourselves nor others. We can get better ourselves, grow, and mature, but such improvement does not come from a focus on fixing anything. Instead of being obsessed about fixing something, the life of an armorbearer is a call to fall ever more deeply in love with God and develop such a desire to please Him that certain habits emerge. These habits then become inspirational to ourselves and others. These habits become contagious. These habits become transformational and, in this way, we grow. This type of life is better caught than taught. So a large part of my purpose will be to encourage us to draw closer to certain examples, both from the Bible and elsewhere, which will increase the likelihood of us catching what God makes available to us all.

I happen to believe that America's story contains some of the best illustrations of servant-leadership the world has ever seen. So, many of the illustrations I use, apart from those in Scripture, will be from the American story.

Once again, I ask you to contemplate who you are, not in the calm, but in the storm. Storms are moments of failure or pain and they tend to be the moments when we learn the most, change the most, and grow the most. These are the moments when we become who we are, and when we uncover the guiding principles for our relationships with others.

A word of caution: do not become enamored with the storm; just let it serve as a backdrop that causes the real you to stand out. Then acknowledge the presence of God with you right where you are, just as you are. Far too many of us spend entirely too much time focusing on our condition in life as opposed to focusing on our opportunity in life. God's presence with us represents our great opportunity to grow and change.

The Apostle Paul wrote, "For when I am weak then I am strong" (I Cor. 12:10). What do those nine words from I Corinthians have to do with uncovering who I am and who I will be in times of crisis? They point to accessing a source of strength centered on something other than myself. This is why the choices made by servant-leaders are revolutionary. Those choices are not the conventional choices for building character and leadership, and they lead in a different direction. Paul's words direct us to a Biblical notion of leadership which, instead of making much of us, makes much of God and the people around us. Our weaknesses and failures can become opportunities for God to be glorified in our lives. It is in our interactions with the work of the Holy Spirit that we gain our strength, and our troubles merely become a stage for the power of God to be displayed. It is exciting to contemplate who you can become no matter how challenging life gets.

There is a good possibility that this journey might become uncomfortable for some of you. I assure you, being uncomfortable is not the worst thing in the world. In fact, it is sometimes a thing much needed. For example, if you are part of a church or just in a relationship with Christ, and you have decided that you will not involve yourself passionately and in deeply committed ways, isn't it time you became uncomfortable with that approach? So much is available to us as Christians, yet we lose touch with that abundance when we focus too much on our comfort.

In John 10:10 Jesus said, "I have come that they might have life and have it to the full." I invite you on a journey of embracing life together in such a way that we inspire each other. How we connect to God and others sets in motion a series of events in our lives that will produce either life or death. If all our interpersonal connections are based only on what makes us comfortable, those connections are likely to lead us into some destructive behavior patterns. Let me illustrate this point with a story.

It was almost one o'clock in the morning when Dr. Leo Winters, a highly skilled surgeon, received an urgent telephone call from the hospital. A child had been badly mangled in an accident and, without immediate help, he had no chance to survive. The doctor took the quickest route to the hospital, which was through a rough neighborhood. When he pulled up to a stop sign, he was stunned when his car door was suddenly opened by a man wearing a grey hat and dressed in a dirty gray flannel shirt, screaming at him. "I've got to have your car!" he demanded as he grabbed the doctor and jerked him from behind the steering wheel. Dr. Winters tried to explain the gravity of the situation—that he was rushing to the hospital. But the carjacker paid no attention. He slammed the door shut and took off in the doctor's car. The doctor was left standing on the street. It took Dr. Winters an hour to get to the hospital, after finally getting a taxi to pick him up. He ran into the hospital only to learn that it was too late. The child had died.

"His father got here a few minutes before the child died," a nurse informed Dr. Winters. "The father is in the chapel. Would you go see him? He is awfully confused. He couldn't understand why you never came." Without saying a word, the doctor swallowed hard, trying to form the words in his mind to explain what had happened. He opened the door to the chapel and there was the father weeping over the loss of his child. The father was wearing a dirty gray flannel shirt and a gray hat.

This father desperately wanted to save the one he loved, but he ended up acting in a way that caused an opposite outcome from the one he desired. There was no doubt that he meant well; there was no doubt about his love; but there was insufficient character development, and an unsupportable behavior pattern, to focus his intentions and his love in a positive way.

- This man had a passion for saving his child's life, but that was not enough to keep him from being part of the problem.

- This man had good intentions and acted on them, but that was not enough to keep him from being part of the problem.

- This man took initiative, demonstrated creativity, and went the extra mile, but he was still such a part of the problem that his actions contributed to an inability to overcome this circumstance. He was a part of the problem even though that was the last thing he ever wanted to be.

This book addresses the deficiency in effective leadership and character formation found in every part of society. We can change programs, plans, processes, and procedures, but if we don't change people (ourselves), we will not experience all that God has in mind for us. By "change ourselves" I don't mean that the power to change comes from us. I mean learning how to embrace the change God seeks to effect in each of us through applying the tenets of servant-leadership as taught in Scripture. Both the Biblical texts that provide crucial guidance in this area and stories that illustrate what that application might look like in everyday life will be our focus.

Most of us are weary of chasing after the latest and greatest self-help plan. The church has seen her share of explosive new growth promises and leaders who "have it all figured out." This is not something new, though it may come across as new to some, due to the fact that we have gotten so far away from the example of Christ. This book is a call to follow the example of Christ. If asked, most people in His day would not have described His leadership as assertive or forward-moving. The Pharisees saw Him as a serious problem, an obstacle to their plans to advance Judaism. In His day, the vast majority of people outside Israel never heard of Him, and the powers in the world at that time took little or no notice of Him. No one stopped His crucifixion or even raised much of a fuss about it. Yet, Christ has changed the world! Why would we search for an approach better than the life of Christ?

Instead of changing programs, plans, processes, and procedures, let's consider changing our place, purpose, power, and passion. Something more is required in life so that we not only avoid unintentionally being a part of the problem, but so we live in such a way that we truly become a part of the solution. We are after the something more in life. Let's go find it, through making the four choices of servant-leadership: the four choices of an armorbearer!

# PART ONE

# I CHOOSE TO LIVE ON HALLOWED GROUND

WHEN WE LIVE ON HALLOWED ground, we are different people. Servant-leaders make the choice to live in a place where God's impact is fully felt and passed along. Hallowed ground is the place where God's presence with us is all we need to make a difference.

Think about it: where we live matters. Our lives are impacted and shaped in significant ways by the place we grew up and the place we live. Just listen to the different languages people speak and the different accents, even within the same language. The customs we adopt, the appetites we nurture, and the things we accept all have something to do with the place where we live. What is true physically is also true spiritually.

Choosing to live on hallowed ground is choosing to encounter God, right where we are, in such life-altering ways that we live differently. One of the great themes of scripture is that God will meet us right where we are, and invite us to follow Him. When we say yes to Him, our perspective changes. Our expectations change, and we adopt a different course in the face of adversity.

In 1 Samuel 14:1–15, we have one of the great, but little known, stories of the Bible. The cast of characters in this story includes King Saul, his son Jonathan, Jonathan's armorbearer, the Israelite army, the Philistine army, and the place where they interact with their circumstances.

> One day Jonathan son of Saul said to the young man bearing his armor, "Come, let's go over to the Philistine outpost on the other side." But he did not tell his father. Saul was staying on the outskirts of Gibeah under a pomegranate tree in Migron. With him were about six hundred men, among whom was Ahijah, who was wearing an ephod. He was a son of Ichabod's brother Ahitub son of Phinehas, the son of Eli, the LORD's priest in Shiloh. No one was aware that Jonathan had left. On each side of the pass that Jonathan intended to cross to reach the Philistine outpost was a cliff; one was called Bozez, and the other Seneh. One cliff stood to the north toward Micmash, the other to the south toward Geba. Jonathan said to his young armor-bearer, "Come, let's go over to the outpost of those uncircumcised fellows. Perhaps the Lord will act in our behalf. Nothing can hinder the Lord from saving, whether by many or by few." "Do all that you have in mind," his armor-bearer said. "Go ahead; I am with you heart and soul." Jonathan said, "Come, then; we will cross over toward the men and let them see us. If they say to us, 'Wait there until we come to you,' we will stay where we are and not go up to them. But if they say, 'Come up to us,' we will climb up, because

that will be our sign that the Lord has given them into our hands." So both of them showed themselves to the Philistine outpost. "Look!" said the Philistines. "The Hebrews are crawling out of the holes they were hiding in." The men of the outpost shouted to Jonathan and his armor-bearer, "Come up to us and we'll teach you a lesson." So Jonathan said to his armor-bearer, "Climb up after me; the Lord has given them into the hand of Israel." Jonathan climbed up, using his hands and feet, with his armor-bearer right behind him. The Philistines fell before Jonathan, and his armor-bearer followed and killed behind him. In that first attack Jonathan and his armor-bearer killed some twenty men in an area of about half an acre.

Then panic struck the whole army—those in the camp and field, and those in the outposts and raiding parties— and the ground shook. It was a panic sent by God. (NIV)

We are introduced to an amazing pair of warriors, Jonathan and his armorbearer, and they end up making an incredible impact. Where did they find the inspiration, the initiative, and the boldness to act when so many around them could not? Is that not a question that needs answering, not just in their time but in our own as well? Not just in their lives, but ours as well? How were they able to see this circumstance so differently from the rest of the Israelite army? I believe the answer has a lot to do with the choice to live on hallowed ground.

All throughout these verses in I Samuel 14, we are given descriptions of the place, the ground upon which these events occur. Everything occurs within the context of an awareness of the ground.

In verse 1 Jonathan says, "Come, let us go over to the **Philistines' outpost** which is on the **other side**."

In verse 2 we are given a description of where King Saul is, "**staying on the outskirts of Gibeah under a pomegranate tree in Migron.**"

In verse 4 specific detail is given about the ground where the armies faced each other. "**On each side of the pass** that Jonathan intended to cross **to reach the Philistine outpost was a cliff**; one was called Bozez, and the other Seneh."

In verse 5 the description of the rocks continues: "One cliff **stood to the north** toward Micmash, **the other to the south** toward Geba."

In verse 6 listen as Jonathan speaks: "Come, let us **go over to the outpost** of those uncircumcised fellows [Philistines]."

In verse 8 Jonathan continues, "We will **cross over** toward the men."

In verse 9 the plan is developed in which place is key. "If they say to us, 'Wait there until **we come to you**,' we will s**tay where we are and not go up** to them."

In verse 10 the plan continues, "But if they say, '**Come up to us,' we will climb up**, because that will be our sign that the LORD has given them into our hands."

In verse 11 we get our first description of how the enemy saw the ground occupied by Jonathan and his armorbearer:, "'Look!' said the Philistines. 'The Hebrews are **crawling out of the holes** they were hiding in.'"

In verse 12 we see the Philistines' plan: "'Come **up** to us and we'll teach you a lesson.'"

In verse 12 we also see Jonathan's response as he says to his armorbearer,"'**Climb up after me**; the LORD has given them into the hand of Israel'."

In verse 13 we have a dramatic description of the ground and its interaction with Jonathan and his armorbearer. "Jonathan **climbed up, using his hands and feet,** with his armor-bearer right behind him."

In verse 14 we see one last description of the place: "In that first attack Jonathan and his armor-bearer killed some twenty men in an **area of about half an acre."**

Verse 15 goes on to describe a great earthquake that occurs simultaneously with the attack of Jonathan and his armorbearer.

What is God telling us with these constant references to the ground? This story could have been told in any number of different ways, focusing on a variety of details, but God chose to acquaint us very well with the ground. Could God have worked in any terrain? Yes, but for God to work through His people, the people of God had to see their ground as hallowed ground. Hallowed ground is hallowed when everything we do is done in response to God.

From these verses we gain some important insights into the perspective of these two warriors, the rest of the Israelites, and the Philistines—a perspective gained from making the choice to live on hallowed ground. From hallowed ground, Jonathan and his armorbearer saw the Philistines in a vulnerable place, suitable for attack. The Philistines occupied high ground but as we will see, it was not hallowed ground. Their place was not a place where they met God, and this changed everything for the Philistines on this occasion.

Saul did not make the choice to live on hallowed ground. Therefore, he was relegated to a place on the sidelines, the place of a spectator. He was the leader, but he was not in a position to lead. He had the authority of leadership but he was not positioned to make an impact using his authority. By the place he occupied, Saul made it almost impossible to make a difference in this situation. Most of the army followed him to this place of passive observance.

The religious leader, Ahijah, looked the part but did not occupy the place. He was wearing his garments of office but he was not performing the duties of his office. He was not making an impact because he did not see himself in a place of impact. He did not even see what he should have been seeing: the absence of Jonathan.

The Philistines were in a place of denial and darkness. They thought they could see clearly that they had the upper hand, but they were blind to the reality of what was happening right before their eyes.

So how did Jonathan and his armorbearer view their place? They saw their ground as hallowed ground. When you see the place you occupy as hallowed ground, you are a different person. Their ground was not hallowed because they occupied it, but because it was where they encountered God. To be sure, we can encounter God any place, but do we usually see our ground as a place of a God-encounter? These two men interacted with God in this place and it changed them and the outcome entirely. Wherever we encounter God, that place is hallowed ground. If we let that truth sink in, we can develop thinking and actions that are inspired.

Genesis 1:27 says, "So God created man in His own image." You bear the image of God, and that means you can make a difference in the lives you touch. In fact, if you are not making a positive difference, you are wasting much of your potential. Making a difference requires a certain mindset and a certain skill set which is available to us as believers. When we live to make a difference in the lives of others, we are best positioned for God to make a difference in our lives.

On the afternoon of April 18, 1775, a young boy who worked at a livery stable in Boston overheard a British army officer talking about a mission the British army was going on the next day, to seize weapons the colonists had stored in nearby Concord. Also, there was some comment about arresting Sam Adams and John Hancock who were hiding in the area. The stable boy ran to Boston's North End neighborhood, to the home of a silversmith named Paul Revere, to let him know what he had just heard. This started the epic ride of which we have all heard: Paul Revere's ride to warn those in danger that the British were coming. What if the stable boy had said to himself, "What can I do? I can't fight the British; I don't even own a gun?" History might have been very different indeed. It is an unfortunate aspect of our times and our Western society that instead of wanting to make a difference, most people today want to be comfortable. The importance of our comfort and convenience is interwoven into our society. It is hard to disconnect from the powerful, shaping influence of the "life is always better when things are easier" mentality. But on hallowed ground, we learn that life is not better when things are easier; life is better when God is present.

Too many people today have no testimony, because they have run away from too many tests. When we embrace life's tests, we gain a testimony with which we can go and make a difference in other people's lives. It is in the midst of life's tests where we most often find God. He meets us there, not only to make a difference in our lives, but to inspire us to make a difference in the lives of those around us.

Jonathan and his armorbearer chose to live on hallowed ground. Those who live in this place find they are amply equipped and consistently emboldened to make a difference. Let's examine several specific ways we can make a difference.

---

To make a difference, use your condition as a part of your impact.

---

In Philemon 1:1–18, a slave named Onesimus has run away and ended up with Paul. During his time with Paul, Onesimus was converted. He accepted Christ as His Lord and Savior. That sounds so simple, yet there are some facts about Paul's condition that we must keep in mind. Paul was a prisoner, and was dealing with the threat of execution. Do you think Paul might have been excused if he had other things on his mind than Onesimus and his problems? Do you think Paul might have been given a pass if he wanted to sit around and throw a pity party for himself? Yes, but he chose to interact with his condition differently.

For too many of us our condition, be it a physical sickness, a relationship struggle, a financial collapse, or, like Paul's, a loss of freedom, sends a message to us: I am a failure. Once we accept that message, all kinds of bad things happen. We lose our confidence, we lose our spark, we lose our passion, we lose our energy, we lose our courage, and we lose our interest in making a positive impact on others. We assume that there is no use in trying. But listen to how Paul speaks in verse 8: "Therefore although in Christ I could be bold . . ." You can tell that Paul does not think of himself as a failure at all, even though he is a prisoner, he has violated Roman law, and he is about to bring the full wrath of Rome down on himself. He is interacting with his condition differently. Someone else not long before Paul also interacted with His condition differently. On the way to the cross, a journey that saw Him beaten, wrongly accused, abused, and mistreated, Jesus did not think things were hopeless. He saved humanity. Jesus and Paul knew how to fail successfully. What I mean is they used their condition as part of their impact. They used what is always in plentiful supply, times of challenge, pain, and hurt, to make a difference in the lives of others.

Your condition buys you credibility. Your condition buys you inside access.

Paul used his condition—he was a prisoner witnessing to a slave. Do you think Paul had some credibility with Onesimus?

Absolutely! Paul's chains and Onesimus' status were the perfect combination. God leads you to the people you are best positioned to impact.

Jonathan and his armorbearer impacted each other and those around them through their mutual experience on hallowed ground. In verse 1 of I Samuel 14, it is to his armorbearer that Jonathan speaks as he prepares to make a difference. It is to his armorbearer he listens as he prepares to make a difference. On hallowed ground, our condition is an opportunity.

---

## To make a difference, identify your current place as something other than ordinary.

---

We have all had the experience of people treating us like we used to be instead of like we are now. This is one of the most frustrating things in the world. We have made mistakes, we learn and grow, and then we still get treated as if we were frozen in time, bound to our mistakes forever. How do we break free from this nightmare? Someone has to come along in our lives and treat us differently—not like we used to be, but like we are now and like we can be. We all need someone who will see us, not as permanently damaged goods, but as people full of promise. We all need people in our lives who can see where we are going instead of only where we have been. If you want those kinds of people in your life, you must be one of those kinds of people for someone else.

Sometimes life on hallowed ground comes with the requirement that we carry another's burden. Are you willing to carry another's burden? Paul, in verse 15 and following, acknowledges that when Onesimus departed from Philemon he was one thing, but now he is another. Verse 16 says, "no longer a slave but . . . a dear brother." Then in verse 18 Paul says, "If he has wronged you or owes you anything, put that on my account." Wow! That is big! Who does that for someone else?

*This is where life-changing impact is made.*

There are so many people who want to get on with their lives but they cannot pay the price they owe, so they are doomed. But you can pay it for them. You cannot do this for everyone at every time, but you can do this for someone, sometime. People need to see themselves differently, and often that begins with you seeing them differently. When people feel as though they are faced with burdens that will never lighten, or they have lost too many battles, or they owe too much, it is not God's fault, and it does not mean that God is disgusted with them.

So many people respond to life by refusing to make choices or refusing to be responsible for their choices. Does it seem like your choices are always limited or made for you by the combination of your condition, your limitation, and your lack of inspiration?

You must be willing to have a different relationship with your condition, whatever that condition might be; this is a guiding vision of servant-leaders. Of all the people in I Samuel 14, the armorbearer is most inspirational. We don't know much about him; we don't even know his name. But what we do know about him sets a clear and unambiguous example of servant-leadership.

Jonathan said to his young armor-bearer, "Come let's go over to the outpost of those uncircumcised fellows. Perhaps the Lord will act in our behalf. Nothing can hinder the Lord from saving whether by many or by few." "Do all that you have in mind," his armor-bearer said, "Go ahead; I am with you heart and soul." – 1 Sam. 14: 6–7 (NIV)

Jonathan climbed up using his hands and feet, with his armor-bearer right behind him. – 1 Sam. 14:13 (NIV)

Obviously, Jonathan is a huge part of this story. But the response of the armorbearer given above in verse 13 is a critical part of Jonathan's life. How the armorbearer responds to Jonathan is so refreshing and revolutionary! Verse 7 is the key verse. The armorbearer responds to Jonathan's statement about what the two of them should do as they are facing an overwhelming enemy in this way: "Do all that you have in mind. Go ahead; I am with you heart and soul." What an answer! This is the response of someone connected to another person in such a way that a positive impact on both of them is sure. With someone like that in your life, you can get things done no matter the amount of failure staring you in the face. This man had something special inside him.

Armorbearers are so valuable because they have a different spirit and perspective in the midst of failure. They have their supreme usefulness when all seems to be falling apart. They transform the ground of defeat into hallowed ground.

---

## To make a difference, embrace leadership as an opportunity to serve others.

---

The story goes that General George Washington was standing before a group of his officers on March 15, 1783, in Newburgh, New York. They were extremely unhappy with the Continental Congress for failing to pay them, among other grievances. They were so upset that they were giving serious consideration to marching on Congress and taking what was theirs and, in the process, doing fatal damage to the fledgling nation. The nation seemed to be on the verge of falling apart.

General Washington addressed his officers by reading from a prepared statement, but his remarks were not being well received. Then something simple yet profound happened. General Washington stopped reading, reached inside his coat pocket, and drew out a pair of glasses. The men had never seen their general wear glasses. As he put his glasses on, General Washington said, "Gentlemen, you will permit me to put on my spectacles, for I have not only grown gray but almost blind in the service of my country."

That small act changed everything. Many of the men began weeping, and their anger abated. They still had issues with Congress, but this moment brought home for them the realization that the war had cost everyone, and this was not the time to throw away the gains that had been won at such a dear price. Why did the act of putting on his eyeglasses make such an impact on these hardened warriors? It was a demonstration of servant-leadership. It was confirmation that George Washington had carried a great burden for them all.

George Washington lived in a seriously status-conscious society, which made the practice of servant-leadership even more difficult in his day than in our own. Nevertheless, he knew something about the principles of servant-leadership, if only innately or instinctively.

Servant-leadership saved the revolution that day and kept the American dream alive. Can such small acts of humility and humanity truly make a difference in our relationships? They can and they do. If relationships drive the human story, then whatever works to make a positive impact is powerful indeed.

The evidence for the need of more servant-leadership is all around us. The deficit in effective leadership is ubiquitous and the impact of poor leadership is alarming. Pride, posturing, and pontificating are what pass for leadership too often, and we all feel the devastating effects. Must we accept that the conditions that gave rise to leaders like Washington, Adams, Lincoln, and Churchill, among others, are gone forever? Certainly our times need truly great leadership as much as any times ever have; therefore, it is important to seek some answers that will hopefully inspire a new crop of great leaders.

The calls for leaders who can make a positive difference are plentiful. Much too infrequently does a leader emerge who gains the trust of the people and is able to get things done. The truth is, we tend to get leaders who are reflections of our inner selves. If we are going to enter a new era of truly effective leadership, we must uncover what it is we are looking for and ask for that in ourselves first. This is where servant-leadership begins—with an examination of ourselves, and a willingness to admit that we need wisdom in this area far beyond the wisdom of man. Listen to what Jesus said on this subject of leadership:

> But Jesus called them to Himself and said to them, "You know that those who are considered rulers over the Gentiles lord it over them, and their great ones exercise authority over them. Yet it shall not be so among you; but whoever desires to become great among you shall be your servant. And whoever of you desires to be first shall be slave of all. For even the Son of Man did not come to be served, but to serve, and to give His life a ransom for many." – Mark 10:42–45

There is a way the world goes about its business, and then there is a way Christians are called to go about our business. There is a way the world deals with failure, and the way people of faith in Christ deal with failure. Making the choice to live on hallowed ground is making the choice to take hold of what God makes available to us. Mark 10 is a central Biblical passage, but there are others, like the passage below, that drive this message home.

> Receive one who is weak in the faith, but not to disputes over doubtful things . . . For none of us lives to himself and no one dies to himself. For if we live, we live to the Lord; and if we die, we die to the Lord. Therefore, whether we live or die, we are the Lord's. – Rom. 14:1,7–8

These verses point us to the definition of servant-leadership. Servant-leadership is leadership that is exercised, not as an effort to make much of the leader, but as an effort by the leader to use his or her position as an opportunity to make much of others and to equip them for service to the glory of God.

The Christian faith is by far the best foundation upon which to build servant-leadership; it is not the only foundation. A central figure in Chinese culture, Lao Tzu, a man who lived between 570 B.C. and 490 B.C., said this:

> The highest type of a ruler is one of whose existence the people are barely aware. Next comes one whom they love and praise. Next comes one whom they fear. Next comes one whom they despise and defy. When you are lacking in faith, others will be unfaithful to you. The sage is self-effacing and scanty of words. When his task is accomplished and things have been completed, all the people say, "We ourselves have achieved it!"[1]

Some might protest that servant-leadership will not work in the military, where command-leadership prevails, nor in the business world where entrepreneurial-leadership prevails. In each case there are goals in place that seem to rule out the practice of servant-leadership. A closer look, however, reveals that military units that function at the highest level are those where the troops are cared for; similarly, businesses that succeed best are those businesses that take care of their people. When servant-leadership is the foundation, it enhances every other kind of leadership.

---

1    *Tao Teh Ching* by Lao Tzu, translated by John C.H. Wu (Boston, MA: Shambhala, 2006)

Listen as these Bible verses continue to deepen the texture of servant-leadership.

*Do nothing out of selfish ambition or vain conceit, but in humility consider others better than yourselves.*

– Phil. 2:3

*Be devoted to one another in brotherly love. Honor one another above yourselves.*

– Rom. 12:10

*Submit to one another out of reverence for Christ.*

– Eph. 5:21

*Humble yourself before the Lord, and He will lift you up.*

– James 4:10

This last verse is my life verse and it speaks to the long history I have with trying to be a servant-leader. Servant-leadership will cause you to ask yourself the question, "But what about me? How do I get ahead by putting others before myself and making much of others?" Good question. The answer is, it's not your concern. God will lift you up; He will look after you. He promises! Matthew 6:33 reaffirms God's promise this way, "But seek first his kingdom and his righteousness, and all these things will be given to you as well."

When I served as a U.S. Marine under President Reagan, at one of our last meetings I was presented an American flag that had flown over Camp David. (This was a custom performed for all those who were departing who had served with the president.)

That moment crystallized for me all the lessons in leadership that I had learned while serving on the president's staff. Observing up close one who had such enormous power, yet who wielded it with such humility, set me on the road to embracing servant-leadership.

---

## To make a difference, be a bridge over bitterness and pettiness.

---

Permit me to return for a moment to another story from the time when General Washington commanded the Continental Army. There was a Baptist pastor, Peter Miller, who was from Ephrata, Pennsylvania. Peter was a friend of General Washington. In Ephrata there also lived a wicked man named Michael Wittman. It seemed that Michael was devoted to making Pastor Miller's life as miserable as possible. One day during the war, Michael Wittman was arrested and charged with treason. He was taken to Philadelphia, tried, found guilty, and sentenced to die. The word got back to Ephrata, and Peter Miller, astonishingly, traveled seventy miles on foot to Philadelphia to plead for the life of Michael Wittman. Being a friend of General Washington, Peter was allowed to present his request in person. General Washington was moved by the sacrificial act, but at first refused the request. He thought Peter was Michael Wittman's friend, which was a reasonable assumption. After all, who would walk that far for a friend? To walk that far for an enemy would never have crossed anyone's mind. But that is exactly what Peter Miller had done, and when General Washington learned of this, it changed everything. Washington knew servant-leadership when he saw it. Michael Wittman had failed miserably, but Peter Miller responded in a way that turned the ugliness of failure into something beautifully inspiring.

A hallmark of a servant-leader is an ability to act in such a way that your actions transcend the pettiness that guides so much of life. No one but a servant-leader would do what Peter Miller did for Michael Wittman. Washington granted the pardon and allowed Peter Miller to take Michael Wittman back home to Ephrata. Between these two men, bitterness was replaced by friendship. This is an example of why servant-leadership is so necessary. It changes lives!

Servant-leadership is a call to invest your life in actions that inspire others. Inspiration is a strange commodity. It requires the fertilizer of hardships. It flourishes in the rains of disappointment. It rushes toward the fires of trouble when all others are fleeing for safety. This is what life is like on hallowed ground. We find ourselves wanting to honor Christ and, in so doing, we begin to take on the burdens of others. For the armorbearer, the burden of making a risky attack was one he accepted with gusto.

On hallowed ground, personal responsibility takes on a whole new meaning. It is an important application of personal responsibility to include our impact on others. Will Allen Dromgoole's poem "The Bridge Builder" captures this essence of a servant-leader well. An elderly man has had to ford a dangerously flooded river because there is no bridge over it. Once he has made it safely to the other side, he stops and, before continuing his journey, builds a footbridge over the river behind him. Another traveler, bewildered by the man's very strange action, asks him:

*"You've crossed the chasm, deep and wide—*
*Why build you this bridge at the evening tide?"*

The man answers him:

> "There followeth after me today,
> A youth, whose feet must pass this way.
>
> This chasm, that has been naught to me,
> To that fair-haired youth may a pitfall be."[2]

We must become passionate about being bridge builders. The life of a servant-leader is not so much about going against the flow as it is becoming a bridge over the flow.

---

## To make a difference, be a conductor of God's power.

---

There was a Scottish discus thrower who wanted to compete in the Olympics. This was a time before Olympic training camps, so he developed his skill alone in the Highlands of Scotland. He even made his own discus from a description he found in a book. What he did not realize was that the discus used in Olympic competition was made of wood with a rim of iron. The discus he made was of solid iron. It weighed four or five times what the wooden Olympic discus weighed. Unaware of his mistake, the Scot trained hard. He marked a field with various distances measured off and he practiced every day. He labored under the burden of the extra weight as he tried to reach the distances. He finally reached a point where he could hit the Olympic record distance

---

2    Will Allen Dromgoole, *Father: An Anthology of Verse* (EP Dutton & Company, 1931), as quoted on the Poetry Foundation website, accessed Nov. 19, 2013, http://www.poetryfoundation.org/poem/237102.

on occasion. The time came for him to leave Scotland and travel to the Olympic Games in London.

When it was his turn to step up and make his first attempt, he was handed a competition discus by the judge. It was made of wood. The Scot was confused, and checked with the judge to make sure this was a correct discus. Upon being assured that the discus was proper, he tossed that discus like a plate. He set a new world record that day.

The key to his success was his preparation, his training. Hallowed ground always includes this crucial part of life. Many of us wear ourselves out trying to do the right thing, but we end up quitting because we did not take seriously our times of preparation.

We must learn the difference between being a source of power and being a conductor of power. In this vein, lots of people are connected to Christ in unhealthy ways. Think of how electricity is delivered. There is a generator: something that produces power. There is also a wire, which conducts the power to cause something to happen. You are a conductor and you have a wire. You are not a generator. The power to be a servant-leader does not come from you. It comes from the One who calls you—Jesus.

A wire is a thin strip of metal to conduct electricity. Christians use a thin strip of faith to conduct God's power. It's not about how big your faith is, but how your faith is being used. Decisive faith focused on Jesus will deliver great power to your relationships with others. Jesus said, "If you have faith the size of a mustard seed, you can say to this mountain 'Move from here to there,' and it will move. Nothing will be impossible for you" (Matt. 17:20). Our faith serves little purpose when we try to be generators. However, our faith works wonders when we position ourselves in line with Christ's power. Servant-leaders are called to be conductors of God's power to the lives of those who need it.

There are three specific rules for being a conductor:

- A conductor does not demand his or her own way.

- A conductor embraces life as part of a family or team.

- A conductor strengthens what he or she has instead of worrying about what is lost.

What is the quality most valued in a conductor? The ability to deliver the power with as little resistance as possible. In conductors of electricity, this quality is found in a certain type of metal. In servant-leaders, this quality is found in a certain type of tolerance. We hear much about tolerance in our society today. It seems as if the more one hears about a subject the more that subject is fraught with misunderstanding and misapplication. Christians exhaust themselves in fighting battles over public displays of crosses, nativity scenes, and the display of the Ten Commandments, all while engaging in unabated, sinful personal behavior. Are we called to tolerate every infringement upon the exercise of our faith? Absolutely not! Are we called to focus intensely on the things that matter most to God? Absolutely! Life on hallowed ground helps us tell the difference.

In the pages that follow, you will meet numerous people from the Bible, from America's past, and from our modern culture, who practiced tolerance. That does not mean they were complacent in the face of injustice. On the contrary, without exception the servant-leaders you will meet acted when few others did. They just didn't exhaust themselves in an endless demanding of their own ways or obsessing over what was lost. They tolerated the imperfections in their own lives and the lives of others because they were focused on something, on Someone, bigger. As you spend time with them, soak in their balance of tolerance with tenacity; take note of the rich texture your character takes on when you take seriously the greatest commandments of all: "'Love the Lord your God with all your heart, with all your soul, with all your strength, and with all your mind,'" and "'your neighbor as yourself'" (Luke 10:27).

To actually live as a servant-leader, we must make some momentous choices in our lives. The other choices we will discuss stem from first making the choice to live on hallowed ground.

# PART TWO

# I CHOOSE TO RISK MY SIGNIFICANCE

YOUR SIGNIFICANCE LIES NOT IN what you gain for yourself but in what you are willing to give away. Servant-leaders make the choice to adopt a purpose for their lives bigger than themselves. Our significance lies in the security of God's provision, and this is the secret to our ability to make a difference no matter the odds. Risking our significance is another way of showing our compassion. Not everyone will respond to compassion. Some people will rebel against any effort at teambuilding or enhancing our fellowship with each other. We should not let the reticence of some discourage us from practices that are highly effective with most.

As we follow the course of making choices that lead to being servant-leaders, we come to our second choice—choosing to risk our significance. This choice is actually a choice to adopt a new purpose for one's life. My new purpose is to apply the security of God's provision in the way I deploy into the lives of others. To operate in this way, I must consider some things very carefully; things such as how have my experiences shaped me, what have my hurts and disappointments done to me, have I come to a place where I know the truth of the Biblical statement, "you meant it for evil but God meant it for good" (see Gen. 50:20).

It is in life's toughest experiences that we gain our true strength, our ability to be tried and tested, dumped on and disappointed. Furthermore, we come out praising God, thanking Him for being with us and praising Him for what He has done in the midst of our storm. Lots of people have experience, but are not better people for that experience. Others have learned to interact with their experiences in such a way that they are better people. This is your significance and God asks you to risk it, to give it away to others through the example you set and the love you practice. Let's examine several specific ways the security of God's provision empowers us to risk our significance.

---

## The security of God's provision empowers us to react differently to suffering.

---

On December 13, 1862, Sgt. Richard Kirkland was part of the Second South Carolina Volunteer Infantry, which was posted along a stone wall on Marye's Heights near Fredericksburg, Virginia. As his unit was attacked by Union forces, those Union soldiers took heavy losses. Many wounded and dying soldiers lay between the battle lines all that night, crying for help. The next morning, December 14, daylight revealed the ghastly scene of over 8,000 Union soldiers lying where they had been shot in front of the stone wall at Marye's Heights. The survivors were suffering terribly from their wounds and from dehydration.

As soldiers from both sides listened to the cries of the wounded, no one dared venture out from their protected positions out of concern for becoming an additional casualty. Finally, Sgt. Kirkland had heard enough and asked for permission to take some water to the wounded Union soldiers. The request was eventually granted with the stipulation that Kirkland not use a white flag. Kirkland decided to take his chances even without the protection a flag of truce might have afforded him.

Sgt. Kirkland gathered all the canteens he could carry. He filled them with water from a nearby stream and rose up from behind the stone wall and went onto the battlefield. Amazingly, he was not shot as he made his way between the lines to the nearest wounded soldier. Both Union and Confederate soldiers watched and no one fired a shot. For more than an hour and a half, Sgt. Kirkland went back and forth carrying water, warm clothing, blankets, and words of encouragement.

Sgt. Kirkland risked his life for those who were not only complete strangers, but also his enemies. Sgt. Kirkland would later lose his life in battle, but, on this occasion, the example set by this armorbearer not only made a difference for those hurting soldiers, but continues to inspire servant-leaders to this very day.

In Mark 8:35 Jesus says, "For whoever desires to save his life will lose it, but whoever loses his life for My sake and the gospel's will save it." Do you want your life to matter? Then servant-leadership is your answer! A word of caution: to some, a call to embrace servant-leadership may seem like resorting to an easy path of risk aversion and political correctness. Nothing could be further from the truth. Servant-leadership is risky and costly and pesky. It irritates pride and proud people enormously. It unsettles the status quo like nothing else. It makes demands on the front end and asks for patience with results.

Another place servant-leadership is reflected is in these words of scripture, "If your enemy is hungry, give him food to eat; if he is thirsty, give him water to drink. In doing this, you will heap burning coals on his head, and the Lord will reward you" (Prov. 25:21–22). No easy path, this journey of servant-leadership. But notice how Proverbs 25:22 closes, "the Lord will reward you." This is why the risk is worth it and why the trouble is bearable. We want to live while we have life in such a way that we make the most of our time.

Who do you want to be? Hopefully you, like me, have a desire to be like Sgt. Kirkland or Jonathan's armorbearer or, more to the point, to be like Christ. The path to such a life is not easy. God confirms this life as His calling for us and He gives us a description of that journey in I Peter 5:10: "And the God of all grace, who called you to His eternal glory in Christ, after you have suffered a little while, will himself restore you and make you strong, firm and steadfast"(NIV). The "you" who is strong, firm, and steadfast is what God calls you to risk through the example you set and the love you practice. This significance is often developed through and after suffering.

Some of us may be thinking that we would rather be the warrior than the armorbearer. Many are thinking, "I would rather be Jonathan and be a prince than someone whose name no one knows." I get that, but let me say this: the best warriors are those who have spent time as armorbearers. The armorbearer must be able to do both, the job of the warrior (notice this man had to fight just like Jonathan) and be able to do the job of supporting the warrior. The best warriors have always been armorbearers also. A classic example is David, who was Saul's armorbearer before he became a warrior-king. Armorbearers show up best when suffering is worst.

---

## The security of God's provision enables us to be significant through serving others.

---

Of course the best servant-leader of all is Jesus Christ. He put so much on the line for us. In Jesus' day, as in our own, leaders were expected to conform to a certain image. That image did not include risking your significance then any more than it does now. Yet Jesus risked His significance, and that is what He teaches us to do. Watch a Master servant-leader at work in John 13:3–5:

> Jesus knew that the Father had put all things under His power, and that He had come from God and was returning to God; so He got up from the meal, took off His outer clothing, and wrapped a towel around His waist. After that, He poured water into a basin and began to wash His disciples' feet, drying them with the towel that was wrapped around Him.

We cannot ignore His example and hope to somehow follow Him. Yes, His path is the path of choosing to risk our significance, but it is not the path of being insignificant. Listen to Philippians 2:5–11:

> In your relationships with one another, have the same mindset as Christ Jesus: Who, being in very nature

God, did not consider equality with God something to be used to his own advantage; rather, he made himself nothing by taking the very nature of a servant, being made in human likeness. And being found in appearance as a man, he humbled himself by becoming obedient to death—even death on a cross! Therefore God exalted him to the highest place and gave him the name that is above every name, that at the name of Jesus every knee should bow, in heaven and on earth and under the earth, and every tongue acknowledge that Jesus Christ is Lord, to the glory of God the Father.

Remember our core passage of scripture, "Whoever of you desires to be first shall be slave of all. For even the Son of Man did not come to be served, but to serve." (Mark 10:44–45). To put this into practice we must first desire to be great (to matter, to make a difference to the glory of God). Then we must make a choice to be a servant. This involves being a slave to all and actually serving. Servant-leadership repudiates victimhood. Making the choice to risk your significance is making the choice to pursue greatness.

Making the choice to risk your significance is not an invitation to be insignificant. It is an opportunity to change the basis of your importance from resting on what you can do, to being based on what Christ can do in and through your life. It is making room for God to work. Most of us can take risks when we are pressed, when the spotlight is on us, when our name is on the line. Making the choice to risk your significance is not about taking a course of action when no other course is available. It is about taking a risk even when you have an easy way out, a ready-made excuse. "Hey, this is not my fight." "Even if I helped out, all the credit and glory would go to someone else." The armorbearer could have easily said, "Go do what you need to do, go ahead. I will be here when you return." And no one would have thought anything about it. But he responded differently. No one is asking you to have all the answers–just don't quit. Serve others to God's glory even when it involves risking what you value, other than your relationship with God. We risk what is significant to us in order to make room for God to work in and through us.

---

## The security of God's provision causes us to pay attention to small yet crucial details.

---

I have faced my share of obstacles. Some of them have literally threatened my life. In addition to serving in the Marine Corps, I served as a state trooper with the South Carolina Highway Patrol. My area of responsibility included South Carolina's coast, in the Pawley's Island area. One night I was on patrol. It was very quiet, with not much going on and hardly any cars on the road. Then I saw a car make a turn and fail to give a turn signal. I thought I would stop this person, have a chat, make a new friend, and pass a little time. It was no big deal, no ticket involved. So I turn on the blue light and pull the guy over. At this point, we were on a back road off the beaten path. I got out of my car and approached his car. I followed the routine of asking him for his driver's license and registration. He fumbled around for some time and finally produced a faded, crumpled California driver's license, which I could barely read. I became a little suspicious at this point and asked the driver to exit his vehicle. He did, but as he was turning to stand up after stepping out of his vehicle, he hit me right in the middle of my face. No warning, no words, just a well-aimed strike to my face. I was stunned. My glasses flew off and my eyes probably crossed. I stepped back and he jumped on me. He got the better of things for several minutes, landing blow after blow as I tried to recover the initiative. At some point I was able to land a few blows of my own. We were grappling together, rolling across the hood of the patrol car, over the highway, into the ditch, back onto the highway.

During the fight he was able to grab the handle of my pistol. He tried to jerk it free from its holster but was unable to do so. It didn't stop him from trying. Later I realized that the belt loops on my trousers had all been ripped loose as my belt was pulled around my body. He said to me as he was pulling at my pistol, "If I ever get this pistol out, I'm going to kill you." I didn't have much to say in response to that. What does one say: "That isn't very nice"? Anyway, we kept fighting and I realized that he was operating under the influence of something (later found to be cocaine) that was giving him an edge in our contest. Late in our fight, I was very fatigued, gasping for air. The best I could do was lie on top of him in the road and hold him down. As I was doing this, I began to pray. This prayer was not my saying anything so much as it was my reflecting on the impressions God was placing in my mind. I remember thinking He was saying, "I am with you." "Relax. There is power in our relationship." Words like this kept flooding through my mind. This was a small detail but with these thoughts, my enthusiasm began to return. (I must admit it had faded a little in the moments late in the fight. I really wanted to be somewhere else.) As we lay there, my cocaine-inspired friend still trying to land blows, my energy began to return. When the thought crossed my mind that God already knew about this man and, therefore, had already prepared me for this moment, I was ready. I flipped the guy over and was in the process of putting hand cuffs on him when a deputy sheriff who had seen my blue light pulled up on the scene and helped me finish the job.

The security of God's provision will cause you to pay attention to details that others overlook. A great obstacle in being a servant-leader will be the protest that "real life" is much too hard to not look out for oneself first. In answer to that protest, I would say that we serve a God who is able to handle real life far better than we can. He is willing to help, if we are willing to ask for and trust His help. The help that God offers has a unique quality of frequently arriving in the small details of life. We see this in three interesting facts about Jonathan and his armorbearer. We learn from I Samuel 14:1–5:

- When Jonathan and his armorbearer left the camp, no one noticed.

- We are not given the name of the armorbearer.

- We are given the names of two jagged rocks in front of Jonathan and his armorbearer.

These may seem like inconsequential details, but they are critical elements in the formation of a servant-leader's attitude. In these details, God is teaching us how to prioritize in such a way as to form the mindset of a true servant-leader.

First, why are we told that no one noticed when Jonathan and his armorbearer left camp? It may have mattered to those concerned with the proper discipline of an army camped in front of the enemy, but why would God want us to be aware of this detail? I think this goes to the heart of the formation of a servant-leader's attitude. So, no one noticed when these two left the camp to save the army. That was fine with Jonathan. The servant-leader is not looking for adulation and adoration. In an image-conscious society such as ours, this is a challenge, but we must have the attitude that we will not be dependent on the acclaim and affirmation of others. (It is nice when we get it, but its absence must never determine our course of action.) The army's expectations for these two men were probably very low indeed. No one noticed their absence because no one expected much from them. This army evidently didn't expect much from itself either. They were in the midst of a stand-off in which doing nothing seemed the best course of action.

I want you to notice something vitally important. Jonathan and his armorbearer did not live down to the expectations of their group or society; they lived up to the inspiration provided by God! And because of what we learn later about the armorbearer, I am convinced that on this occasion the inspiration from God poured through the armorbearer and inspired Jonathan. The armorbearer had an attitude that is still refreshing across all these centuries.

Also, we are never given the armorbearer's name. To many of us this might seem like a cruel oversight. If in fact the armorbearer played such a crucial role in what was about to transpire, surely God would have given us his name. Having one's name up in lights is proof of one's importance, so we are led to believe. Well, in real life, where true impact is made, the real heroes always make it about someone else. True servant-leaders are most at home not being called out, not being recognized. True servant-leaders are never concerned about their own glory and recognition. It is altogether fitting and proper that this armorbearer is never named.

How do we develop attitudes like this man had? We need to stop worrying about our own glory (as difficult as this may be). We need to redirect the passion we have for building ourselves up and instead to using our gifts from God to honor God. We need to find greater fulfillment in the awesome privilege of being a part of the great work God is doing on this earth. We need to live with a greater awareness of that moment when we will stand before Christ and hear His words, "Well done, good and faithful servant" (Matt. 25:21).

Benedict Arnold was one of the best combat leaders in the Revolutionary War, on either side. He was courageous and bold in battle. He inspired his men and he got results. Like other leaders on the American side, Arnold experienced his share of setbacks in combat, but he also played an integral part in some decisive victories. His leadership was pivotal to the American victory at the Battle of Saratoga. Benedict Arnold was a great combat leader. But he was not a great servant-leader. Even while contributing greatly to the American victory at Saratoga, he was quarreling with his commander, General Horatio Gates. Arnold lived for the acclaim of man. Arnold felt that he never received enough rewards or recognition, and this character flaw ruined him.

General Washington saw General Arnold's value as a combat leader, and he tried to address issues related to Arnold's "me-centered" approach to life. After Arnold was wounded in battle, Washington gave him the best assignments available to a general who could not take the field. However, commands in Philadelphia and at West Point failed to be the stepping stones to a better outlook on life for Arnold. Washington took some risk in appointing Arnold to these important positions, a fact made clear by Arnold's treason in trying to give West Point to the British. Yet Washington did not miss his opportunity to try to provide some help to someone he valued. Can you identify and utilize the stepping stones that God provides?

Speaking of stepping stones, this brings us to the final detail—we do know the names of the two jagged rocks standing before Jonathan and his armorbearer. We do not know the armorbearer's name, but we know the names of two rocks. This seems a little incongruous at first, as if God's priorities are out of order. But the reverse is actually the truth. Those stones, which will become stepping stones, at first appear as obstacles. Why would God name the rocks and tell us their names—Bozez and Senah—and their exact locations? To make an important point. If God gives names to your problems, then they are under God's control.

This changes the nature of your problems entirely. If your problems are known to God and under the control of God, they have ceased to be stumbling blocks and have become stepping stones. Your problems are then stripped of some of their mystery and darkness. Fear of the dark is built on fear of what cannot be seen. God is saying that your obstacles are seen as clear as day by Him, so trust Him and don't be afraid.

With this revelation, you are freed to assess things in an entirely different light. The rocks that had halted both armies became markers for the trail that Jonathan and his armorbearer followed to victory. The security of God's provision was clearly evident in the midst of their challenge.

The fruit of choosing to risk our significance is a clear connection to God's provision. When we have the issue of our provision settled, we are then able to build on that in our relationships with others.

---

## The security of God's provision empowers us to build relationships based on trust.

---

When my son Mitch was very young, I would sometimes take a walk with him through our neighborhood. After some time of walking and talking, taking turns down one street after another, when I was sure he had no idea how to get back home, I would stop and ask him, "Mitch, do you know how to get home?" He would answer honestly, "No." My next question to him was, "Well, doesn't that make you afraid?" His answer to me was as refreshing as it was revealing. "No Dad, I am not afraid; you know the way home." He said it with such surprise: that I could not see the reality of his situation and how there was absolutely no need for fear. Now if there was a spider around somewhere, maybe there would be a need to be afraid; but not knowing the way home when you are with your Dad: that's a piece of cake! My relationship with my son was built on trust. For his part this trust was rooted in his confidence in my ability (my provision) to get us back home. Should it not be even more so in our relationship with our heavenly Father?

So often our trust is built primarily on the way other people behave. We cannot ignore this reality completely. But even when dealing with those whose unintentional behavior is untrustworthy, we can build a trust connected to God's provision. In fact, people who unintentionally act in untrustworthy ways might need our trust more than anyone else.

Trust is missing from many relationships today. The air is filled with skepticism concerning those who lead us. This is not unjustified, given all the leaders who have failed. Having acknowledged that fact, we must not, though, take the attitude that all leaders are unworthy of our trust. Nor must we conclude that every failing in a leader constitutes sufficient reason to withdraw our trust. Neither Jonathan nor his armorbearer was perfect, but this did not preclude a relationship built on trust. Trust has always been, and always will be, the glue that holds people together. When trust is absent, relationships deteriorate, and unity of purpose and action become almost impossible. When trust is absent, people refuse to be risk-takers. America at her best is a nation of risk-takers. If we lose this characteristic, we will lose an essential quality of the American character.

We see the importance of trust in I Samuel 14:6. "Jonathan said to his young armor-bearer, "'Come, let's go over to the outpost of those uncircumcised fellows. Perhaps the Lord will act in our behalf. Nothing can hinder the Lord from saving, whether by many or by few.'" Notice he said "let us go." Jonathan assumed that his armorbearer had his back and would go into the thickest part of the fight with him. There was no discussion of where the armorbearer's proper place would be. There was no look in the armorbearer's eyes that said, "I'll be right here waiting for you when you get back!" There was no wondering or worry on the part of Jonathan about his armorbearer. Of all the uncertain things swirling around them in that stressful time, the armorbearer was a rock. Trust was evident in their relationship.

Servant-leadership is built on trust. We trust each other not because any of us is perfect, but because we have learned to develop different expectations in our relationships. We see life not as an individual pursuit but as a family affair. If I do not allow for any alternative but sharing life with you, then I am highly motivated to make our relationship work. Our relationship is not disposable, it is essential.

Therefore, servant-leaders equip others to make a difference through their victories and strengths, while also encouraging them to grow from their mistakes and weaknesses. Trust is given a chance to take root and grow as we engage in life as a collaborative effort. Let me suggest some ways that trust is valuable, by sharing some of the ways trust is built.

**A servant-leader builds trust through using *compassion*.** Compassion is a powerful leadership tool that engages people emotionally, and investment in the heart is just as important as investment in the head. A person receiving compassion is likely to champion the right thing when it comes time to help others in need. Good leaders know that people make mistakes. Mistakes, however, do not change the fact that every person is sacred.

**A servant-leader builds trust through using a context of *commitment*.** When you know that someone is committed to you, you feel enabled to be honest, motivated to try harder, and inspired to serve smarter. Servant-leaders are defined by what they give rather than by what they take. You've probably heard the term "take-charge leader." I would like for you to consider a variation on that term, give-charge leader. For give-charge leadership to work, people must know that taking chances and making changes are possible and that mistakes made along the way are not catastrophic.

**A servant-leader builds trust through using a *vision*.** Visions often sound very compelling. Yet visions are risky, and leadership should not seek to soft-pedal involvements that run the risk of failure. Good leaders do not ignore this or act as if it does not exist. Trust in a vision stems first from trust in God, and then in the people God brings into your life.

**A servant-leader builds trust through using *teamwork*.** How can you convince everyone on the team to take responsibility for the entire team's performance? Help them understand that each team member is vital to the other's success. Teamwork embraces the notion that no work is unimportant, and no one is too important to do whatever needs to be done. This is a practical kind of leadership, which stresses solving real problems instead of merely doing things that feel good. Trust is undermined by the call to engage in busy-work: work that leads nowhere. Trust overflows in the midst of a spirit of teamwork, where people share together the challenges of life and the struggles involved in pursuing a dream.

Let's expand on this subject of building trust, by looking at another key phrase in I Samuel 14:6: "nothing restrains the Lord from saving by many or by few." When you are part of the few, outnumbered and surrounded, trust becomes a powerful and much-needed companion. Normal leadership functions well when the odds are in our favor, but it often falls short when difficulties mount. It is no small point that, for most of us, life is full of the odds not being in our favor, so we need leadership and character formation sufficient for the realities we face in life.

Jonathan and his armorbearer could have failed; indeed, they should have failed. They were two going up against hundreds. But they had a relationship built on trust. They chose to be driven by something other than fear of failure. They chose to act on the fact that God can work through unknowns and "out-numbereds," as well as He can through well-knowns and massive numbers. The clear evidence of Scripture is that God does His best work when we are weak. Thus, the servant-leader Paul spoke these words, "That is why, for Christ's sake, I delight in weaknesses, in insults, in hardships, in persecutions, in difficulties. For when I am weak, then I am strong" (2 Cor. 12:10).

This theme continues throughout Scripture, as servant-leaders choose to risk their significance because they trust God and those God has put in their lives. God sent most of Gideon's army away (see Judges 7:2–3). God instructed the Israelites to march around the walls of Jericho (see Joshua 6). These are not the normal actions of people who want to succeed. Such actions have great potential for making one look foolish. But they were willing to risk their significance, go against conventional wisdom, and declare their trust in doing things God's way. God is always intent on getting His people focused on Him, as opposed to focused on the possibility of failure. Many people don't set goals and don't take on greater challenges in an attempt to reduce the risk of failure. Servant-leaders opt for a different path. Risking our significance for the glory of God is the path of greatness. Trying to hold on to our significance and hoping to mitigate the chance that we will fail is the path of misery.

Consider Jonathan's father, King Saul. In chapter 14 of 1 Samuel, we learn about Saul and the path he chose. Saul was not a servant-leader, and we see that clearly in his actions here.

- Saul failed to communicate well with his son (v.1).

- Saul failed to take action when the Philistines were routed (v.19).

- Saul failed to ask for God's help ahead of time (v.19).

- Saul failed to recognize that something could be done in spite of overwhelming odds (verse 20).

- Saul failed to control his emotions and made a rash vow, resulting in his troops being unprepared for battle (v.24).

Saul's problem was fear of failure, and it destroyed his life. He would not risk his significance, and so he ended up losing everything. He would not trust in God or the people God placed in his life.

Jonathan and his armorbearer followed a different path. They approached their obstacles and fears remembering that God's hand was not restrained in their lives. God routinely works through things we discount and things we try to forget.

When we build relationships on trust, they bear the mark of God's presence. This is what servant-leaders know. Building relationships on trust is indispensable. The arrival of an armorbearer invites the formation of a relationship built on trust. That would be enough, but there is even more available to us when we have the confidence of God's provision.

---

## The security of God's provision energizes us for action even when resources are limited.

---

God will call you to do something, and often it will seem as though He has left you pitiful little to work with. It is tempting to respond to this reality by using this as an excuse for giving up. His provision might seem to be too little, but this is never the case. God offers us the option of His provision in place of our own so that we will be forced to depend on Him and learn to trust Him. Shamgar is a servant-leader you probably have never heard of. The Bible says in Judges 3:31, "After him was Shamgar the son of Anath, who killed six hundred men of the Philistines with an ox-goad; and he also delivered Israel." An ox-goad is a stick used by farmers to herd oxen; it is not a weapon of war. So the God-given provision for Shamgar was a stick. He used a thin stick to kill 600 Philistines. Now, I ask you, if you were given the job of killing 600 Philistines, would an ox-goad be your weapon of choice? Most of us not only want to serve God, but we want to look good doing it. In fact, the fear that we might not look good serving God, that we might even look foolish, causes many people to make themselves unavailable to God. You ask God for help and He gives you a stick. Now what will you do? Will you trust in God's provision even though the resource seems limited and might make you look foolish to the world? God blesses His plan. And His plan always includes His provision.

George Washington, Thomas Jefferson, John Adams, Abraham Lincoln, and Martin Luther King Jr. were all leaders who were discontent with the status quo. It is easy to look back across history and say, "Yes, action was required." Yet, too often we don't see our own issues that require decisive and sacrificial action. We can see why others needed to take action, but too often such action never seems to be part of our own lives. We never seem to be in a situation that warrants our risking our significance. With this mindset, we pass our days opting for the dull hum of the road well-traveled instead of the sacred ground where one person looks at another and says, "Do all that is in your heart. Go then; I am here with you, according to your heart" (1 Sam. 14:7).

The armorbearer believed the situation warranted a sold-out response. Such a belief is born out of a passionate discontentment with the way things are and the faith that we have enough resources at our disposal to take action.

Jonathan and his armorbearer were not content with the way things were, as the army of God just sat there in front of the army of the Philistines. This sounds like the situation when David was a young boy, standing up to Goliath. In each case, the threat was huge, and the available resources appeared small. This is why most people will not take action, and why Martin Luther King Jrs. are so rare.

Does it often seem to you that no matter how much you would like to change things, your hands are tied by a lack of available resources? A priceless element of servant-leadership is the capacity to keep going when the odds are stacked against you. This is possible when you stay focused on God and others instead of on yourself. This focus connects you with God's provision and enables you to identify circumstances worthy of your taking enormous risks. Don't miss doing what you can do right now, just because the odds seem prohibitive. These famous lines from an old Scottish ballad, "Sir Andrew Barton," capture a servant-leader's mindset when in the midst of severe trials:

> *I am sore wounded but not slain.*
> *I will lay me down and bleed a while*
> *And then rise up to fight again.*

Jonathan and his armorbearer faced daunting odds—odds long enough to deter even the stoutest of hearts. Let's follow along as these two make their decision to act. First, note that Jonathan and his armorbearer did not resort to calling a meeting. They did not even inform the king. They did not look to pass the buck. Nor did they depress themselves with an unending review of the problems they faced. Jonathan made a decision to act based on the information and the resources he had available.

Let's take an inventory. Jonathan did not have an army at his disposal; all he had was his armorbearer and a belief that the occasion warranted decisive action. Additionally, he was not content that the army of the living God should be stopped by the Philistines or the terrain. This discontentment was shared by his armorbearer and (I would submit) in large measure instigated by his armorbearer. When Jonathan said to his armorbearer, "let us go and perhaps God will work for us," he did not have to explain himself to his armorbearer. They shared this discontentment and desire for taking action. They did not doubt whether God would act. They were leaving room for God to define the victory, but there was no fear of failure, which stops so many from acting.

Let's consider Saul, the conventional leader, further. I Samuel 13:7 says the people "followed him trembling." Saul's fear of failure opened the door for fear to spread throughout the people.

Saul's use of conventional leadership doomed the whole army to indecisive inaction at a time when action was required. This fear and inaction spread, to the extent that Saul made a rash vow and worked at cross purposes with what God was bringing about in this situation.

Having pointed to the failings of Saul and conventional leadership, it must be recognized that taking action when facing longs odds is not for the faint of heart. It takes much focus and prayer, as well as trial and error, to become a risk-taking, decisive servant-leader.

Because the Bible goes to the trouble of providing us significant details regarding how the armorbearer responded to Jonathan, I think we can conclude that the armorbearer's response was crucial. Jonathan was a good man and well-intentioned, but it is likely that nothing would have been done had the armorbearer responded differently. Had his armorbearer said, "Jonathan, I don't think we can do this," it is very likely that Jonathan also would have lost heart. Instead, the armorbearer responds, "Do all you have in mind. Go ahead; I am with you heart and soul" (v. 7). What an inspiration this must have been for Jonathan! What a stark contrast this attitude represented compared to everyone else, from the king on down.

The armorbearer replied to Jonathan by offering all that he had—his heart and soul. When someone offers you their heart and soul, you must take notice. This is what armorbearers do. They offer others their heart and soul, and then plunge into the fray with them and rejoice in the work of God. The arrival of an armorbearer gives rise to discontentment with the way things are and infuses others with the belief that positive change is possible, because someone is willing to offer their heart and soul. But we are not yet done with the treasures unleashed in a servant-leader's life when he or she has confidence in God's provision.

---

The security of God's provision ensures vision to see the path to victory amid life's adversities.

---

The impact of an armorbearer is at its greatest when opposition is at its worst. The great thing about being an armorbearer is that it gives you a unique perspective on your obstacle, your opposition. Some people are surprised by the level of opposition they meet in life. This is especially true when you are focused on being a good person, playing by the rules, and treating others as you would want to be treated. Suddenly, POW! You get hit right in the face with anger, bitterness, gossip, and all the rest that people can do to each other. When you add to this the unpredictable nature of things, such as sickness and negative circumstances largely beyond our control, adversity is a considerable presence in life. Armorbearers are required to perceive and remember the weakness of adversity. When disconnected from God's plan, purposes, and power, any adversity—whether it goes by the name of Goliath or cancer—is powerless to overcome God's will. Something that may seem at first an impossible obstacle, upon reflection becomes ripe with opportunity.

I call your attention again to that armorbearer turned warrior-king, David. The entire Israelite army was stopped by a Philistine giant named Goliath (see 1 Sam. 17). There seems to be a pattern here of the army being stopped in its tracks by adversity. David, a shepherd boy at that time, is the one who steps up to take action. Outwardly, David was a child. He could hardly pick up Saul's armor, much less bear it. But inwardly his heart was focused on God. His passion was for his Lord, and this shaped him and everything around him. David was able to sense, by the power of that same God he loved, that Goliath's imposing exterior disguised an empty interior. Goliath was rotten to the core. Love of self was at the center of what drove Goliath.

During the stand-off, it is interesting that David was criticized by his brother and probably others for (allegedly) showing up looking for attention, or maybe to collect the ransom, or the hand of the King's daughter that Saul had offered. But these were not the rewards which inspired David at all. They very likely were the kinds of things Goliath was pursuing.

Have you ever said to yourself, "if I could only see this person or this situation more like God sees"? This is the perspective that servant-leaders learn to adopt, through the grace of God. A comparison between the perspectives of conventional leadership and servant-leadership is useful at this point. I Samuel 17:33 tells us that King Saul, the conventional leader, saw a little boy with no battle experience taking on a giant who had been a skilled warrior from the days of his youth. King Saul says in verse 33, "You are not able to go up against this Philistine."

Compare that with what David, the servant-leader, saw. 1 Samuel 17:26 tells us what David saw: "Who is this uncircumcised Philistine, that he should defy the armies of the living God?" See the difference? David was able to act when no one else could because he saw the weakness of his adversity. David loved God passionately, and this meant he could easily recognize the absence of a love for God. Love for God was not in Goliath's heart. Pride, arrogance, greed, lust, and conceit were the driving passions for Goliath. Against such decadent passions, God wins every time!

One final thought on David as he faced adversity; he was the one who was willing to take action and he was also the one who was most severely criticized by those closest to him. That is always the most severe kind of adversity. We expect criticism from our enemies, but we are never quite prepared for criticism from our friends and those close to us. But David is able to overcome even this and accomplish what God had called him to do. David focused on his purpose instead of his problem. David focused on his cause instead of on his critics.

In verse 29 of 1 Samuel 17, David cries out, "Is there not a cause?" This is indicative of his vision. The others could see only the overwhelming strength of an obstacle. David could see only serving the cause of God and the resulting weakness of the adversity when compared to that cause. David could not see Goliath like the rest of the Israelite army did, because God was in the way. Don't we all need to let God get in the way more often? When God gets in the way wonderful things happen!

We have some phrases that have come down to us through the centuries, which serve as markers for when people acted heroically and overcame enormous adversity because they saw something others could not. The phrases still inspire us as they cascade through time:

"I have not yet begun to fight!"

"Don't fire until you see the whites of their eyes!"

"I regret that I have but one life to give for my country."

"Thy servant will go and fight with this Philistine."

The question is not, how could such people have such courage? For "uncommon courage is a common virtue" for every person—large or small, young or old, rich or poor—who is shaped by God into a servant-leader.

Now, let's return for a moment to the scene from I Samuel 14, in which Jonathan and his armorbearer are ready to take action. We see that the Philistines are ready to oppose Jonathan and his armorbearer. Oh, you thought that because these two had demonstrated such faith and such resolve their opposition and adversity would melt away? Not so. That's not what happens in real life. What is your experience when you walk by faith? Trouble is always ready to take a stand. Verses 11 and 12 record the words of the Philistine adversaries: "'Look!' said the Philistines. "The Hebrews are crawling out of the holes they were hiding in." The men of the outpost shouted to Jonathan and his armor-bearer, 'Come up to us and we'll teach you a lesson.'"

Too often we prepare and we pray and then we expect our obstacles to be immediately removed by God. If we look up and see the obstacle is still there, we must be prepared to take action and engage. For this to work, we must be able to see something to exploit, some weakness in the adversity that will give us a foothold. Instead of focusing on what was against them, Jonathan and his armorbearer focused on Who was for them—God. This focus gave them their perspective into their adversary's weakness. In verse 10 we are told how this works: "But if they say, come up to us; we will go up for God has delivered them into our hands." Jonathan and his armorbearer centered the issue on God's presence. They would act in concert with the will of God. When we act in concert with the will of God and we see that which is in disobedience to the will of God, we have identified a weakness in our adversary.

Yes, my enemy is strong and he is ready, but he is not concerned with bringing glory to God. Yes, my weaknesses are significant, but I am partnering with God. No one person ever does this perfectly, and sometimes our commitment to following God will waiver as we try to adjust to all that life throws at us. But if we will work to regain a focus on bringing glory to God, it will vastly improve our perspective and our prospects for success. Armorbearers learn to function in the shadow of the Almighty. Yes, two men against hundreds or thousands seems hopeless . . . if we leave God out of the picture.

Verses 13 and 14 tell us that Jonathan and his armorbearer climbed up the hill. Can you imagine what the Philistine soldiers must have been thinking? One minute they were calling out their insults, resting comfortably in their hubris, and then they noticed the two figures making their way up the hill toward them at a steady, determined pace. No matter how confident you may be, when you see two men full of faith, courage, and humility before the Lord coming your way, the thought will occur to you, "Hey, these guys mean business!" The two kept climbing ever closer. "Do they realize they are only two, and we are two thousand?"

It is not the two who make the difference. It is the God of the two. Your adversary—your adversity—has met its match in the God you serve. Just keep climbing. Don't concede defeat before the battle is even joined. The armorbearer is crucial in moments like this, where the obstacle is not moving out of the way. It is the armorbearer who sees enough to keep going, with the confident trod of someone who sees more than what is visible.

Twenty Philistines fell at the first contact. Then verse 15 tells us, "Panic struck the whole Philistine army. . . . It was a panic sent by God." When you find out that someone actually hates you or that some difficulty is not going away easily, this information can be a little unsettling. When you have identified your purpose in life and you set out to live that purpose, yet not everyone is cooperating, that can be disappointing if you are not prepared. Make up your mind that you will see and respond like someone who has already been delivered by the Lord. You may not know how or when, but your God is invested in your success. He paid a Cross-worth of investment. Maybe you have not considered what God is doing behind the scenes; maybe you have not put weight to what it means to have God's presence in the midst of your storm, but it is a huge thing indeed!

When God is present, we cannot help but be impacted with the passion of His heart, which is a heart for people. Hebrews 10:24 says, "And let us consider how we may spur one another on toward love and good deeds." There is a neat word that captures the idea of spurring one another on: holistic. Holistic means "interconnected." A good example of both the presence and the absence of holistic relationships, and how they change a person's perspective on adversity, comes from the life of Jacob Duché.

Jacob Duché was pastor of Christ Church, in Philadelphia. On September 7, 1774, he delivered the first-ever prayer before the Continental Congress. John Adams wrote, "I must confess, I never heard a better prayer." The story continues. On July 4, 1776, Jacob met with the leadership of Christ Church to decide whether or not to pray for the king in the upcoming Sunday service. In the politically charged world of Philadelphia, excluding prayers for King George was potentially deadly. They made their decision. Today you can visit Christ Church and see in the 1776 prayer book where an ink line crosses out the prayer for the king. Rev. Duché led his congregation to take a bold stand. But there is more. Later, when the British occupied Philadelphia, Duché was arrested. Under duress, he wrote a letter to General Washington, who was camped at Valley Forge, urging Washington to surrender to the British! Duché went from hero to outcast.

Duché had drawn strength from his small group of leaders and, when he was separated from them, it made a big difference. Community is critical! You are not the same person when you are not connected to others. Connect to others on the basis of your willingness to sacrifice for them, as opposed to how it may advance your own interests.

I'm a member of several small groups, and they all enrich my life and make me better. Recently in one of the groups, Carl shared a story that beautifully illustrates the importance of our connections. Carl showed us a picture of a train engine hooked to a coal car, which in turn is hooked to a caboose. A man is standing on the coal car. He has a shovel in his hand and he is shoveling coal into the caboose. Now the engine represents Truth. It is the Word of God. The coal car represents faith. It is the fuel we use to activate the Word of God in our lives. The caboose represents feelings. It is the emotional side of life, revolving around what we want and what we like. If we use our faith to feed our feelings, then nothing happens. Our feelings do not improve. But if we use our faith to feed our interaction with God's Word, then we move, we make progress. If we will focus on the facts of God's Word, we will grow and our feelings will follow; they will improve.

When you are surrounded by people who are able to sharpen you, not only are you stronger, but you are able to see the obstacle before you. None of this happens, however, without our willingness to risk our significance and to be a part of something bigger than we can be as individuals. We will talk in more detail in the next chapter about love, but its importance in everything we do cannot be overstated. We risk what the world tells us never to put at risk—ourselves—because of love. When we do, we find that love is central to so much that we had been looking to find. Watch as this process is recounted biblically:

So that Christ may dwell in your hearts through faith. And I pray that you, being rooted and established in love, may have power, together with all the Lord's holy people, to grasp how wide and long and high and deep is the love of Christ, and to know this love that surpasses knowledge—that you may be filled to the measure of all the fullness of God. – Eph. 3:17–19

Risking your significance does not seem like such a great risk when we see more clearly the outcome. The greater risk is run by whoever chooses to operate with something other than God at the center of their endeavor.

If all our interconnectedness is based on self-advancement, then we end up working against each other. What is good for me may at times not be good for you. If our interconnectedness has as its source of strength each of us only doing what we want to do, the bonds that tie us together are easily broken. If we cannot find something stronger to hold us together, we will fall apart in the face of opposition.

One of the most important things people who propose to work together can ever do is to be clear about what calls them together from their separate interests. This was the genius of the men who wrote and spoke at the time of our nation's founding. Men such as Thomas Jefferson, John Adams, Thomas Paine and Patrick Henry were able to articulate a reason for being interconnected. Here are just a few words from Thomas Paine:

> We have this consolation with us, that the harder the conflict, the more glorious the triumph. What we obtain too cheap, we esteem too lightly; 'tis dearness only that gives everything its value. Heaven knows how to put a proper price on its goods; and it would be a strange thing indeed if so celestial an article as freedom should not be highly rated.

Paine is identifying the pursuit of freedom as the thread that connected the colonists. In the process, he is giving the people a vision of the path to victory amid an unending call for sacrifice.

Paine is doing something else in this quote above. He is pointing to an attitude among people that connects them more tightly than just about anything else—a mutual willingness to pay the price required for victory, for friendship, for the chance to make a difference. King David also knew the power of personal investment in another person, and how a shared willingness to pay the price of putting oneself at risk for another was so valuable. On one occasion, some of David's friends risked their lives to procure a drink of water for him during a long, hot battle. "So the three mighty men broke through the camp of the Philistines, drew water from the well of Bethlehem that was by the gate, and took it and brought it to David. Nevertheless he would not drink it, but poured it out to the Lord." (2 Sam. 23:16). Why did David respond like this after his friends had risked so much for him? Indeed, his actions seem very strange to us who have grown up in a culture that stresses the value of getting all we can with as small a price to pay as possible. Such an attitude is useful, but by his action, David was declaring that the water was much too valuable for his personal consumption. This water was used as an offering of praise and gratitude to God, the God who inspired men to be courageous and unselfish, the God who adds great value to our lives through our mutual willingness to risk our significance for each other.

King David knew what he was doing. Often we lose our boldness for decisive spiritual action, for sacrificing our significance, because we are not sure what we are doing, because we are not sure about our life's purpose. The value of a holistic small group is in being surrounded by people who know me and who can help me understand what I am doing with this thing I have called "faith in Jesus."

There is an African word, *ubuntu*, which means that I can only know myself as I see myself through your eyes. This is a call to gain something other than a subjective, highly biased perspective on our lives. A friend is a treasure beyond compare when we need objectivity about ourselves.

*"A friend loves at all times. A brother is born for adversity."*
– Prov. 17:17

*"As iron sharpens iron, so one person sharpens another."*
– Prov. 27:17 (NIV)


If we can learn to inspire each other to take risks and act in unselfish ways, we will uncover a treasure that will be of value in every relationship. Can you refuse the temptation to focus on your circumstances at the cost of the people in your life? Will you stop listening to those voices of doom? When hopelessness is present, will you respond by reaffirming your hope in God?

You may have heard the phrase, "Give a dog a bad name and he'll live up to it." We tend to live up, or down, to the label that we have accepted as definitive in our lives. Most people are not living anywhere close to their full potential, because they cannot move past how they see themselves. In John 5:1–15, we see another example of someone who could not see the weakness in their adversity. Jesus' response in this situation is of great value to every servant-leader.

> Some time later, Jesus went up to Jerusalem for one of the Jewish festivals. Now, there is in Jerusalem near the Sheep Gate a pool, which in Aramaic is called Bethesda and which is surrounded by five covered colonnades. Here a great number of disabled people used to lie—the blind, the lame, the paralyzed. One who was there had been an invalid for thirty-eight years. When Jesus saw him lying there and learned that he had been in this condition for a long time, he asked him, "Do you want to get well?"

"Sir," the invalid replied, "I have no one to help me into the pool when the water is stirred. While I am trying to get in, someone else goes down ahead of me."

Then Jesus said to him, "Get up! Pick up your mat and walk." At once the man was cured; he picked up his mat and walked.

The day on which this took place was a Sabbath, and so the Jewish leaders said to the man who had been healed, "It is the Sabbath; the law forbids you to carry your mat."

But he replied, "The man who made me well said to me, 'Pick up your mat and walk.'"

So they asked him, "Who is this fellow who told you to pick it up and walk?" The man who was healed had no idea who it was, for Jesus had slipped away into the crowd that was there.

Later Jesus found him at the temple and said to him, "See, you are well again. Stop sinning or something worse may happen to you." The man went away and told the Jewish leaders that it was Jesus who had made him well. (NIV)

According to the Bible, an angel descended into the pool of Bethesda and stirred up the waters. When this occurred, the first person who could get from the porch into the pool was healed. While this was a blessing to the one person who could get in, it held disappointment for everyone else who was desperate for healing. One day, as the sick and infirm were lying there waiting on the waters to move, Jesus passes through. Don't run past that simple statement, "Jesus passed through." Jesus passes their way.

Jesus places Himself within their reach. Jerusalem holds nothing but conflict and trouble for Jesus at this time, but he is unconcerned about the risk to Himself; He comes to the people anyway.

Notice the difference between Jesus and those at the pool of Bethesda. The people at the pool are waiting. They are surrounded by disease, and everything in their circumstance shouts "victim." They are living up, or down, to the name "hopeless."

The man lying at the pool is the epitome of helplessness and hopelessness. Here is a man who is unable to do for himself. He has to be carried everywhere he goes. He is forced to beg his way through life. He is desperate, and with no vision to see any crack in his adversity.

Jesus is the other one present at the pool that day. What a difference. He comes to the place where the sick, the lame, the weak, the outcast, and the hurting are, and He does not see their situation as they do. He is not waiting. He is placing Himself within their reach so that hope might take the place of hopelessness. Jesus does not ignore those who are hopeless or those who are hurting. He loves them and risks His significance for them.

Jesus chooses to go to this pool. He doesn't have to go. It doesn't sneak up on Him. He doesn't stumble by. He knows what He is doing. He is going to this pool the same way He went to Samaria to find the woman at the well, and the same way He went to find the nobleman who had a sick son. The same way He came to find you. Jesus moves toward need, not comfort. He moves toward brokenhearted sinners, not the self-righteous. Jesus will place Himself within your reach. He does not require you to be whole or able or first. He does not require that you figure everything out.

He just requires you to respond to His love. Will you respond like a person who is loved by God, and believe that Jesus has arrived to change everything about your circumstances?

The crippled man had a plan: lie by the pool and desperately hope that someone would help him into the water. Jesus had a better plan for the man and for each of us. He comes to us to offer us life and hope right now, right where we are, because He loves us. All we have to do is respond to His love! This is the pattern for all servant-leaders.

Verse 5 says the man had been at the pool for thirty-eight years. How could someone follow a course of action that fails and disappoints for so long a period of time? Many people tend to do what they can do and then stop. What if what you can do is not enough? Do you know how to access something bigger than yourself? Do you know how to be captured by a bigger vision than "woe is me"? This man's problem had become the biggest thing in his life. His problem had become a way of life for him. Notice what happens when our problems become a way of life:

- Problems as a way of life become the excuse for our complacency and idleness.

- Problems as a way of life take from us the desire to get up when we are knocked down.

- Problems as a way of life cause us to waste too much time looking for someone else to blame.

- Problems as a way of life turn us into obstacles for others.

- Problems as a way of life limit our vision of what is possible.

- Problems as a way of life become a bad name that we try to live down to.

In verse 6, we see Jesus as He begins the process of helping the man break free from living life with his problems as a way of life. Jesus says to him, "Do you want to be made well?" At first this might seem like a silly question. Of course the man wants to be made well, and of course Jesus knows the man wants to be healed. The man has been lying by the pool for thirty-eight years. But as the man responds to Jesus' question, we begin to see what is happening. In verse 7, the sick man answers Jesus with a presentation of his problem. He says no one will help him and every time the water is stirred, another beats him to the pool. But Jesus was not asking him what his problem was. Jesus was asking him if he wanted to be made well. The sick man's problem had become a way of life in which, day after day, he tolerated the existence of a problem that seemingly had no solution. When Jesus asked him if he wanted to be made well, Jesus was telling the man to declare an emergency. Declare a state of emergency in your life and it will change the situation you are in—because it will change you.

As long as we merely make the best of things but refrain from declaring a state of emergency, we accommodate the status quo and nothing ever really changes. What will change when we declare a state of emergency? Our lives will be impacted by the Word of God more than by our feelings. The Word of God is not for keeping things the way they are! The Word of God is for rescuing the perishing, giving sight to the blind, and making the lame to walk again—the kind of stuff that requires a state of emergency.

Verse 8 says, "Jesus said to him, 'Rise, take up your bed and walk.' No more waiting, no more hopelessness, no more problems as a way of life. Once the man declared that a state of emergency existed, once the man cried out that he needed help now, he was ready to drink deeply when he was offered living water. Instead of waiting for the water to move, he was moved by the words of Jesus Christ—"Rise up!" Verse 9 says, "And immediately the man was made well, took up his bed and walked." The word of God is powerful, sharper than any two-edged sword. Respond to it, be moved by it, and your life will never be the same. This is the message servant-leaders live by and carry to all who will listen.

It would be wonderful if the story ended with verse 9, but there is more. And this more is the stuff of real life for us all. The man is healed and happy for the first time in at least thirty-eight years; then he encounters some religious people. They are happy for him, right? No, they challenge him! Verse 10 records their response: "It is not lawful for you to carry your bed on the Sabbath." What! Can you believe this? Well, yes. Most of us can, because we have first-hand experience with not just the hostility of the world but with the hostility of our friends and those who should be encouraging us. There is a lesson here. If you are only after the gifts and healing of God and not a relationship with God, you will not be able to stand the trials that follow those good moments in God's Word.

*Religion and good works alone will fail you.*

– Eph. 2:8–9; Titus 3:5

*Being a good person alone will fail you.*
– Matt. 19:17; Gal. 3:22

*Family associations alone will fail you.*
– Phil. 3:4–9

*Church affiliation alone will fail you.*
– John 3:3,7

We must not just get up. We must get up, walk by faith in Christ, be connected to God's provision, and be ready to connect with others. Jesus healed the man and disappeared before the man could find out who He was. He didn't even know who healed him. Does this mean Jesus had no intention of dealing with this man's soul? No. The man is asked, and he tells them he does not know who healed him. Later, in verse 14, Jesus finds him again and tells him to walk by faith, to stop sinning lest a worse thing happen. You see, being healed, being helped by God can be followed by an even worse thing—separation from Christ for eternity. This is why we must be moved by the power of God not just to help us or heal us, but to transform us into new creatures who live to glorify Christ Jesus the Lord. Verse 15 says the man departed and told the Jewish leaders that it was Jesus who had healed him. When you know Jesus, there is only one thing to do—tell it, so you can bring glory to His name. This is what servant-leaders live for in life.

Jesus warns the man that, if he turns away, and mocks this gift, or makes an idol out of his health, and embraces sin as his way of life, he will perish. This man has a different name now—he has been rescued by the living Lord and King—Jesus Christ. He has a new name to live up to. Servant-leaders are committed to living up to the Name of Christ and encouraging others to do likewise.

Making the choice to risk your significance is not reserved for those times when everyone understands what you are up to and will applaud your deep devotion to Christ. On the contrary, the choice to risk your significance will usually be exercised when few understand what you are doing, when many will speak evil of you for doing it, and suffering will likely increase because of it. 1 Peter 4:1–16 speaks of this reality and begins with the language of war: "arm yourselves."

> Therefore, since Christ suffered in his body, arm yourselves also with the same attitude . . . As a result they do not live the rest of their earthly lives for evil human desires, but rather for the will of God. For you have spent enough time in the past doing what pagans choose to do . . . They are surprised that you do not join them in their reckless, wild living, and they heap abuse on you. But they will have to give account to him who is ready to judge the living and the dead. . . . Above all, love each other deeply, because love covers over a multitude of sins. Offer hospitality to one another without grumbling. Each of you should use whatever gift you have received to serve others, as faithful stewards of God's grace in its various forms. If anyone speaks, they should do so as one who speaks the very words of God. If anyone serves, they should do so with the strength God provides . . . do not be surprised at the fiery ordeal that has

come on you to test you, as though something strange were happening to you. But rejoice inasmuch as you participate in the sufferings of Christ. . . . If you are insulted because of the name of Christ, you are blessed, for the Spirit of glory and of God rests on you. If you suffer, it should not be as a murderer or thief or any other kind of criminal, or even as a meddler. However, if you suffer as a Christian, do not be ashamed, but praise God that you bear that name. (NIV)

When you risk much because of the name of Christ, you are blessed. This is a statement of fact that may not be echoed in how you feel at the time. Therefore, be ready. Think differently. We serve one who has already risked much more than He will ever ask us to put at risk. If risking my significance is the price for more of Christ in my life, am I willing to pay that price?

Permit me to expand for a moment on how we are blessed when we risk much in the name of Christ. Our willingness to live life in this different way, risking our significance, positions us where Christ lives. It is a sure way of participating in closer fellowship with Christ. Christ lives in places of greatest need and places of strategic importance, places most others want to avoid because of the danger. My friend and pastor, David Day, recently discussed one such place, the rearguard, in a sermon. David told the story of one of Napoleon's generals, Marshal Ney. As Napoleon made the decision to withdraw from Russia, Marshal Ney was given the job of leading the rearguard. The rearguard is composed of those soldiers who will risk everything so that the bulk of the army can get safely away. As the main army turns its back on the enemy, to escape, it presents a vulnerable target that invites attack. The rearguard accepts this reality and is willing to live where desperation, intense pressure, and seemingly long odds are facts of life. Long after the main army was safely back in France, so the story goes, some officers were sitting around in a tavern speaking of the recent battles and campaign they had endured. One of them brought up the rearguard, which none of them had given much thought to since their safe return home. They had assumed that the rearguard had been wiped out by the enemy. As their conversation continued, the door to the tavern opened and there stood a French general in a tattered uniform. It was Marshal Ney. Shocked at the sight, one of the officers asked, "General, where is the rearguard?" "I am the rearguard," Marshall Ney replied. Upon hearing that reply, the officers stood and applauded the General. We recognize the honor and blessing of those who live by such a set of values and principles as to make an impact on others at great personal cost to themselves.

Servant-leaders choose to risk our significance, because we operate in the presence of One who is much more significant than us, and who is worth every sacrifice we could ever make. What we put at risk out of obedience to Christ, we find returned to us many times over in the overflowing power and love of Christ in our lives.

You are secure in Christ. The kingdom of God is well; resources are unlimited and available. Generosity should be your mindset and gratitude your motivation. Risk becomes investment and challenge becomes opportunity. Making the choice to put your significance at risk becomes a "reasonable act of service."

# PART THREE

# I CHOOSE TO SPEAK REDEMPTION

CONVENTIONAL LEADERSHIP SAYS "ACT STRONG." Servant-leadership says "be strong." Servant-leaders make the choice to tap into the power of redemption. All throughout Scripture, God speaks to us using a very powerful language: the language of redemption. To understand God we must understand redemption. Do you speak redemption?

For many people, love is a way to describe the feelings they have for someone or something they are attracted to. Such feelings seem to be very strong. But this kind of love fails over and over. It is almost comical, the number of people who profess their love for each other one minute and are fighting like bitter enemies the next. If love has true strength, surely we must look elsewhere. Have you ever been part of a love that promised much but delivered little? Love is unable to keep people from divorce; love is unable to overcome divisions and differences on too many occasions. What are we missing?

We are missing that unique quality of love that causes one to do the right thing even when the right thing is the hard thing. We are missing that quality of love that causes one to sacrifice all for an enemy. This kind of love is foreign to most people's understanding. It is not foreign to God. The Bible speaks of love this way:

> *But I say to you, love your enemies, bless those who curse you, do good to those who hate you, and pray for those who spitefully use you and persecute you.*
>
> – Matt. 5:44

> *For when we were still without strength, in due time Christ died for the ungodly.*
>
> – Rom. 5:6

Conventional notions of love merely position us to respond well when someone treats us well. As we have seen from the verses above, there is much more to love than that. Redemption concerns itself with the real power of love. Redemption centers on the action of God towards us. He gave His Son to die for our sins when we were still unlovely and incomprehensibly ugly to Him. God loves us not because we are good, but because He is good. God shows up in the midst of our mess and speaks to us in a way very different from what we might expect. He speaks to us words of forgiveness, of a second chance, of a fresh start, of unconditional love. God speaks the language of redemption. We must speak that language as well.

Redemption is love that is practiced, not due to the worth of the recipient of our love, but due to the worth of the God who loved us first. This is unconditional love. This is love with real power. This is the power of redemption. We can all love when we are attracted to someone or something. But can we love when our love must be expressed in the face of enormous odds: odds that will very likely cost us immensely? How did Jonathan's armorbearer become a person who was able to respond in the way he did, even given the huge odds they faced? How was he able to love unconditionally when it looked like it would cost him his life? What had shaped his character so that he could step up when it would have been so easy to pass the buck or run away? Redemption; he spoke redemption. Let's examine several specific ways the language of redemption guides our ability to love unconditionally.

---

## Redemption brings power sufficient to pay the cost of discipleship.

---

The cost of discipleship is "He must increase, but I must decrease." (John 3:30). It is a cost we must be willing to pay. To decrease is not a call to lose influence, but just the opposite. To decrease is not a call to pay and get nothing in return; in fact the return is greater than the payment. To decrease is not a call to hate my life, instead it is a call to experience the abundant life offered by Christ.

1 Corinthians 13:1-13 sounds the call to battle:

> If I speak in the tongues of men or of angels, but do not have love, I am only a resounding gong or a clanging cymbal. If I have the gift of prophecy and can fathom

all mysteries and all knowledge, and if I have a faith that can move mountains, but do not have love, I am nothing. If I give all I possess to the poor and give over my body to hardship that I may boast, but do not have love, I gain nothing. Love is patient, love is kind. It does not envy, it does not boast, it is not proud. It does not dishonor others, it is not self-seeking, it is not easily angered, it keeps no record of wrongs. Love does not delight in evil but rejoices with the truth. It always protects, always trusts, always hopes, and always perseveres. Love never fails. But where there are prophecies, they will cease; where there are tongues, they will be stilled; where there is knowledge, it will pass away. For we know in part and we prophesy in part, but when completeness comes, what is in part disappears. When I was a child, I talked like a child; I thought like a child, I reasoned like a child. When I became a man, I put the ways of childhood behind me. For now we see only a reflection as in a mirror; then we shall see face to face. Now I know in part; then I shall know fully, even as I am fully known. And now these three remain: faith, hope, and love. But the greatest of these is love. (NIV)

Love is the greatest because it connects us with the power of redemption. Redemption instills discipline in the way we love. I have been bought with a price by the sacrifice of a Savior, so how could I shrink from the lesser price I am asked to pay for making a difference in the life of another? Redemption sets our value. We are each worth the price of the life of God's only Son. So the challenge to decrease so that we might serve others is no threat to our own value. Our value is set through our redemption.

---

## Redemption brings power to overcome our fears.

---

We were created to live in fellowship and relationship with God and each other. This is a fearful proposition, given the damage that is done in and through many relationships. We need the power which comes from redemption through our faith in Christ if we are going to flourish amid intimacy.

What is a sign of true intimacy? Is it not when you give someone the right to tell you the truth even when the truth hurts? Is not a true friend one who has earned the right to say whatever needs to be said and you will listen? To be strong involves functioning in relationships in such a way that we have earned the right to be heard. This is love in action and it has its birth in how we relate to God.

Our fears are transformed through the power of redemption. The "fear of the Lord is the beginning of knowledge" (Prov. 1:7a). This refers not to our being in terror of God, but to our allowing the wisdom of God to form a boundary for our behavior and choices, which keep them from dishonoring God. Boundaries of righteousness, of holiness and justice, of self-restraint and service are good things to have in our lives. We need to be reminded of them continually.

What passes for love in so many cases is actually hypocrisy. We can say one thing and do another out of fear. Love is crippled in the process. Armorbearers practice a love that is formed to overcome fear. The idea for the servant-leader is to speak words of encouragement which are tied to more than the outward appearance, words which consider inward sincerity and motivation. Few people, probably including the Pharisees, intentionally set out to be hypocrites. Usually it happens as a result of developing some bad habits. Our passion for the Lord may dim or grow cold. In response, we continue to go through the spiritual motions and outward form of religion but never get around to addressing what is really going on in our hearts. We end up going nowhere, like the Israelite army before the Philistines. Servant-leadership is always going somewhere: taking us to a place where God's wisdom is heard and heeded even when the message is uncomfortable.

Fear in our relationships is so devastating because it opens the door to Satan. Satan is highly invested in love being abused, misused, and underrated. Leaders who follow Satan's lead in being uncomfortable with love cannot be strong: they may act strong, but they cannot be strong.

In relationships, we must take responsibility for helping each other, not judging each other. Job 24:2a says, "There are those who move boundary stones. (NIV)" We move boundary stones, warning signs, so that we can do whatever we want to do and still try to act as if our actions meet with God's approval. A servant-leader does something much more than merely point out that a boundary has been crossed: servant-leaders build relationships in which people can be reminded, warned, encouraged, and redirected. This is unconditional love.

Strong and healthy relationships bear a unique quality. They are marked by each person treating the other as better than himself or herself. Are you willing to make an investment of yourself so fully that you end up treating another person as if they were more important than you are?

---

## Redemption brings power to put others first.

---

To treat another as better than oneself is perhaps the most revolutionary thing a person can do in life. It is not easy. It is not natural. It cannot be done without supernatural help. This is why it is so important. It is an approach to life that demands that we seek God's power. Whatever requires us to cling more tightly to God is a good thing. Those who can do this become a beacon in the middle of darkness.

My son Matt is going through a growth spurt. He is becoming a different person. He is seeing different things. He is much more interested in eating these days. He makes comments like, "Dad, you are not as tall as you used to be." One of the ways he handles all the change in his life is by locating and keeping contact with a constant in his life. I am the constant he compares himself with to judge his progress. Servant-leaders are willing to express love through being constant, reliable, and a known element, no matter how much the winds of change are blowing.

Remember our core passage of scripture: "And whoever of you desires to be first shall be slave of all. For even the Son of Man did not come to be served, but to serve" (Mark 10:44–45a). To put this into practice, we must first desire to be great (to matter; to make a difference to the glory of God). Then we must make a choice to be a servant. This involves being a slave to all and actually serving them. Servant-leadership repudiates victimhood. Making the choice to love unconditionally is making the choice to pursue greatness.

Speaking redemption is not an invitation to be unloved or abused. It is an opportunity to change the basis of your love from being how you feel and how others treat you, to being based on what Christ can do in and through your life when you love others. It is making room for God to work. Servant-leaders are willing to be revolutionary in their relationships with others. This means we put others first. The language of redemption instills courage for such a course and establishes a context in which putting others first becomes a reasonable course of action.

---

## Redemption brings power to give our all to what matters most.

---

We tend to do only what we must; we get involved up to a point, but rarely do we give our all to anything. Have we become masters at cloaking our half-measures in religious busy-work? Are we content with the appearance of power, but no actual power? Do we reason to ourselves, "even if I gave it my all, what difference would that really make in the big scheme of things? I am only one individual."

There is a nautical phrase that is helpful when considering that loving unconditionally means giving our all to what matters most. The phrase is "nail your colors to the mast." It comes from a custom practiced in the days when sailing ships did battle.

If during the course of a battle a ship was ready to surrender, it would lower its colors (another name for its flag). This meant the other ship would cease fire. However, if a captain decided that there was no way he would surrender, for whatever reason, then he would take the ship's flag and nail it to the ship's mast so that it could not be lowered. This action made an indelible statement upon the crew of his ship and the enemy ship. In the approaching battle, there would be no surrender, no half-measures, no quarter asked. It was a simple yet unmistakable sign of total commitment.

When our love for others is marked by this "nail your colors to the mast" kind of commitment, we cannot help but make an unforgettable impact. Loving in this way is stripped of all preconditions, post-conditions, unforeseen conditions, and it becomes unconditional. The result is that there are no layers between us and the object of our unconditional love.

When Jesus made His way to Jerusalem for the last time, He knew what was ahead. Yet He steadily made His way there, in spite of the approaching pain and suffering. It takes enormous focus and devotion to willingly place oneself in harm's way for another. In John 12:25 Jesus says, "He who loves his life will lose it, and he who hates his life in this world will keep it for eternal life." How can Jesus speak this way? There is nothing in this verse about our rights and privileges. There is nothing about our being affluent or comfortable. There is nothing here about making much of self. But there is a lot here about finding life. Losing one's life often goes hand-in-hand with feelings and experiences of failure. Letting go of "me first" can feel like failure. Perhaps the hardest thing about letting go is that it so often does feel like failure.

Focus on what matters most: God and the power of God at work in the lives of people. For with God, all things are possible. But as we know, this is not an easy attitude to adopt when we face huge obstacles. So we must strip away as much self as we can from the equation. By "self" I mean thoughts such as: "God should do this for me; it's only fair." Or "I am a good person, why would God let this happen to me?" These questions emerge from the complications caused by a "me first" approach to life and love.

Luke 12:13 and following relates a story in which Jesus was walking through a crowd and someone approached Him and wanted Him to settle an inheritance squabble. There was no preparation for a miracle; there was no trusting in God to take care of him; there was no walking by faith. For this man, what was most important was what he wanted, and Jesus was just a pawn in his effort to get what he wanted. In this way, Jesus became not God, but an estate planning lawyer. This is why Jesus responded the way He did: "Man, who made Me a judge or an arbiter over you?" This man did not want God; he wanted his financial inheritance. While thinking of his due, he forgot his debt. When we forget our debt to Christ, we lose our faith in His ability to change our lives. A great inheritance was lost as this man complicated his life through obsession over a lesser gain. The man chose to ignore the enormous gift of God standing before him, while trying to scrape up the crumbs of a financial inheritance. The money was limited, whereas faith in Christ is unlimited in its potential—and it is unforgettable!

Life has little joy when we are beguiled into believing that success can mean only "me first." Jesus issues a warning in verse 15: "Take heed and beware of covetousness, for one's life does not consist in the abundance of things he possesses." Success is not found in the possession of things, but in one's ability to love God and others unconditionally.

---

## Redemption brings power to overcome failure.

---

Jonathan and his armorbearer were willing to risk massive, public, and life-ending failure because they were unafraid of failure's presence in their lives. They were familiar with the opportunity that arrives hand-in-hand with every moment of failure. With such an attitude, much can be accomplished for God.

Fear of failure often hinders our faith. This need not be the case. Let your moment of failure be a call to focus on Christ. He is with you in your moment of failure and offers much in return for the price you are paying, if you can look away from your destructive focus on your failure and look to Him. In this process, you unleash an unstoppable faith in Him.

So many people miss out on learning important character lessons because they do not want to fail. But speaking redemption to others requires a certain familiarity with failure. This is not a call to live life recklessly or to not take certain reasonable precautions. We do not need to invite failure. It will come of its own accord. The call to speak redemption to others is a call to stop obsessing over your status, you being in control, and you having it all together. What matters most is not that I have failed, but how I respond to my failure. Can I refrain from the urge to make it all about me?

Spiritual success will remain elusive until and unless we close the gap between the words we speak and the actions/behaviors we engage in (the love we express). How do we close the gap? You might not like the answer. It is by appreciating the lessons to be learned in times of struggle. Redemption has great value because we are not what we can be without it. Spend a season in a spiritually dry and dark place, a place where you see yourself clearly, a place where your redemption is not a minor brush-up but a major reclamation project. Then, when your pursuit of God becomes something more than a religious nicety and instead becomes the desperate cry of a desperate person seeking what only God can provide, you are ready to speak redemption to others.

---

## Redemption brings power to propel us to victory in the midst of death.

---

We all want victory, but few of us want the desperation that often precedes victory. In servant-leadership, God is teaching us to process the dryness and the darkness differently, so that we are able to love others unconditionally. In the midst of our pain, we learn to use our tongues in praise to Him instead of using our tongues to express bitterness. The result is a depth of character much greater than we ever knew. When this happens, a huge blind spot is eliminated and we see hardships as we have never seen them before. The result is fruit born not of broken emotions but of deep roots in Christ!

February 3, 1986, was not a typical day for me. I was in law enforcement and was assigned to escort the McNair family on the day of Ron McNair's funeral in Lake City, South Carolina. Ron was an astronaut on the space shuttle Challenger, which exploded shortly after takeoff. Ron had seemingly had it all in life, and his death was a shock to his family and friends, as well as to the country. As I listened to the comments that day, there was deep grief, but there was something else. There was anger and bitterness. Some there were unwilling to accept what had happened. The suffering and loss had no satisfactory explanation, and that was causing people to settle in a bad place, to settle for less than was available to them. Their hearts seemed to be captured by a spirit of rebellion and bitterness over the impossibility of regaining what they wanted most. For some, the celebration of a life well-lived was lost and overwhelmed by sadness over what this death meant for those who were still living.

Trying to describe that day, I would characterize it as seeing some people settle outside of God's presence. It was not that God was not available; to be sure, He was. But it was that there was such a spirit of rebellion. There was a lack of submission, and the result was people making a choice to settle outside God's presence. They seemed to prefer a place where they could indulge in negativity. Can it be that people would prefer to settle in a place where they could wallow unrestrained in anger, grief, and self-centeredness? Yes, it can; I saw it that day.

Redemption makes it impossible to settle outside of God's presence. It compels us to seek refuge in God's presence. Redemption reminds us that there is more power in God's will than in my will. I can demand my way, but have I counted the cost?

The way of Christ is clear:

*Whoever wants to be my disciple must deny themselves and take up their cross and follow me.*
– Mark 8:34b

*If anyone desires to be first, he shall be last of all and servant of all*
– Mark 9:35b

*Submitting to one another in the fear of God.*
– Eph. 5:21

*Let each esteem others better than himself.*
– Phil. 2:3b

Yes, God is everywhere and His grace is always available, but a person can choose to demand his own way such that the result is repudiation of God's offers of assistance. An example of this comes from the Old Testament. Israel decided to go to Egypt in a time of crisis and thus settle outside of God's presence. God responded this way in Jeremiah 42:15 and 16: "If you wholly set your faces to go to Egypt, then it shall be that the sword which you feared shall overtake you there in the land of Egypt . . . and there you shall die." In spite of God's warnings, the temptation to settle outside of God's presence is a strong one when we are guided by how we feel and what we want. Let's refuse to settle for less than God's best.

---

# Redemption brings power to conduct ourselves with less attachment to this world.

---

A sojourner is someone who adopts a certain mindset. That mindset is captured in verse 11a of 1 Peter 2: "Beloved, I beg you as sojourners and pilgrims"; here believers are called "sojourners." As aliens and strangers, not tied to the ways of this place, we are free to keep moving until we get all the way home.

Our love cannot be at its strongest when we are in bondage to things other than God. Many of us not only don't see ourselves as sojourners on this earth, we don't want to see ourselves this way. A deeper look at this issue might cause us to reconsider. A sojourner does not have the mindset of a native. The sojourner does not feel compelled to adopt the customs and standards of the country he is passing through: it is a foreign country. A sojourner is always aware that he is going somewhere else and is, therefore, less swayed by the allure of the country he is passing through. To settle in this place would be to settle in a place that is not home. If we adopt the mindset of this place, we make ourselves strangers to God. Sojourners don't get too attached to the country they are passing through.

There are two benefits in not being too attached to this place:

- Sojourners do not invoke a fight-to-the-death mentality over everything. Freed from the need to fight every battle, we then have energy to focus on the example Christ set for us to follow. Sojourners can practice unconditional love, because they have not expended so much energy propping up the appearance of having mastered the game of success inherent to this place. I will find my security and my sense of belonging, my sense of being home, when I make much of God—not when I make much of myself. Home, in the spiritual sense, is found as we make much of God. When I fight every small battle that comes along, I become a small person. We are called to decrease that He might increase, but we are not called to be petty. This is how unconditional love is practiced.

- Sojourners are not so focused on their rights. This world is not our home, and with this mindset comes different expectations. Like the millions of immigrants who have come to the United States over the years, we are focused on opportunities much more than rights. (It is only later generations who transitioned to a greater focus on rights.) Sojourners value the great opportunity to glorify Christ in this place, where so many settle outside of God's presence. This is how unconditional love is practiced.

In this world you are going to fail, be misunderstood, be taken advantage of, lied to, and lied about. The question is, how will you respond to these realities? Some will fight every battle large and small that comes their way. No slight will be too small to warrant an all-out attack in response. But is this the honorable course? Sure, it may make us feel better when we give as good as we get, but is that really our main goal—that every person who tangles with us knows they were in a battle? God indicates for us a different priority in today's Scripture. Our conduct should be honorable in a way that points others to Christ even as they are in mid-attack on us. The question then becomes, how will I fight?

I recommend the power of redemption. At its core, redemption is about love. Love is the answer for the Christian, but it is an answer that needs some explaining in the context of conflict. This is where the cost of discipleship comes into play. We have already discussed how we are free from a "fight to the death" mentality, but that does not mean we do not fight. We do. We just fight differently.

As Christians we are not simply foreigners; we are in enemy territory. In a sense (don't take this analogy too far, however), we are surrounded. Not only are we surrounded, but because we are all still "in the flesh," we feel the tug of temptation emanating from within: covert infiltrators are at war with us. So the war has been joined on all fronts, and we cannot succeed by force. Force has been tried by Christians during the Crusades and the Inquisition, in addition to the many small ways of manipulation and intimidation of others that we attempt in our daily lives. The enemy hopes we will resort to his tactics, but God has given us a better response. When we fight evil on evil's terms, we are fighting an unwinnable war. When we fight evil on God's terms, we are fighting a war in which the victory has already been won through Jesus Christ. So how do we fight on God's terms? We speak redemption. We love as God loves us.

---

## Redemption brings assurance that our treasure is safe.

---

In conflict, the great threat is that one side is going to attack and take something of value from the other side. Such a threat must be met with force. Fighting on these terms is an unwinnable war for Christians living on the earth today. Instead, love changes the terms of our fight. Love is a declaration that the thing of greatest value in my life is my relationship with Jesus Christ.

He is my treasure, and my relationship with Him is beyond the reach of any enemy.

Romans 8:33–39 states clearly that our treasure is safe:

> Who shall bring a charge against God's elect? It is God who justifies. Who is he who condemns? It is Christ who died and furthermore is also risen, who is even at the right hand of God, who also makes intercession for us. Who shall separate us from the love of Christ? Shall tribulation, or distress, or persecution, or famine, or nakedness, or peril, or sword? . . . in all these things we are more than conquerors through Him who loved us. For I am persuaded that neither death nor life, nor angels nor principalities nor powers, nor things present nor things to come nor height nor depth nor any other created thing, shall be able to separate us from the love of God which is in Christ Jesus our Lord.

If the thing you value most—your relationship with Christ—is safe, then you are free to respond in a way that points people to Christ. You don't have to fight to look good, or defend your honor, or avoid failing so that you always look good. This is fighting a winnable war. People can be persuaded if you are persuaded. What is the evidence that I am persuaded, that I am secure in Christ? I am willing to love.

When we love unconditionally, we declare the complete sufficiency of Christ in our lives! This frees us to think about others in a more favorable and generous light. We are empowered to stop using our freedom to try to get what we want (we already have what we want) and instead of taking care of ourselves (we have already been well cared for), we can "honor all people. Love the brotherhood. Fear God. Honor the King" (I Pet. 2:17).

God is clear about the most important indicator of success and victory, the most important proof of our value, the most necessary ingredient for our hope—God is with you. You are part of God's plan of redemption. This means that for you, victory looks like God never leaving you or forsaking you. Victory looks like, not the absence of problems or messes, but trusting God in the mess to work in ways that accord with His plans and purposes. Victory looks not like the accumulating of things, but the chance to know Christ more and deeper with each passing day.

---

## Redemption brings power to embrace humility.

---

Humility is the most effective energizer of servant-leadership that God has placed at our disposal. To gain humility, we do not strive to be humble: that inevitably leads to more pride. Yes, people can actually be proud of their humility! Inevitably, if we are not careful, even our serving will somehow be about us. We see this unfortunate fact of life evident as far back as the disciples. James and John, the sons of Zebedee, and their mother asked for Jesus to grant them a wish. They wanted exalted positions on Jesus' left and right. They had been serving Jesus, but their request betrays serious problems with their service.

Self-righteousness and self-serving are not what Christlike service is about at all, yet not only do we see it in the disciples, we see it in ourselves. We want to be acknowledged; we want to be coddled; we want to know what's in it for us when we serve. These things are natural, but when they become preeminent, we are in spiritual difficulty. To this, then, we turn our attention. How do we shape and sharpen our service so that it declares without equivocation the glory of God? How do we put the "servant" in servant-leadership? This is what making the choice to love unconditionally is really all about: not how we feel, but what we do.

We shape and sharpen our service through avoiding a spirit of manipulation in our service. We have all faced the temptation to practice some form of manipulation to get what we want out of others—and then we call this "serving God." We can easily intertwine a spirit of manipulation with our faith and convince ourselves that we are serving the cause of Christ. But are we really?

Notice how James and John's mother approaches Jesus. She kneels down before Him. She has the appearance of humility. It reminds us of those moments in our lives when we give the appearance of being team players; we feign unselfishness and concern for the greater good when in actuality we have an agenda. In this way, our service is defined by our wants. This is not how to practice the spiritual discipline of Christlike service. In fact, this practice of service, with a heavy dose of manipulation trying to accomplish what we want, is highly dangerous, in that it can convince us that we are in the right and anyone who disagrees with us is not only wrong, but unspiritual.

How many times have we served God or others in His name, yet come away with feelings of disappointment or frustration, jealousy, or disillusionment? These feelings are common wherever the spirit of manipulation is working hand-in-hand with our service. What causes a spirit of manipulation to intertwine itself with our sincere desire to serve the Lord? Often it is a feeling of entitlement. When we think we have earned something (i.e., a bigger salary, more respect, a spot on the left or right of Jesus), then we begin looking for that something.

Service is not about looking for something; it is about an opportunity to do something out of gratitude for what has already been done for you! Jonathan and his armorbearer were motivated to act, to serve, out of gratitude to God.

Instead of a spirit of manipulation, be guided by a spirit of abundance. As believers in Christ, we have been given so much more than we could ever expect; should that not leave us in a state of perpetual gratitude and thanksgiving? Do we not realize how blessed we are already? A spirit of manipulation robs us of the joy of our salvation; it strips our service of its true value. Instead of being a thank offering, our service becomes a down payment on convincing God to do more for us. God needs no convincing or manipulation. He is already releasing to us more blessings than we could ever imagine. We are wealthy in the spiritual sense and, therefore, our service should be an extension of our wealth, not an extension of our fear of being seen as poor or weak or a victim, nor as a tool to gain something. You are the rich man or woman, so be generous in serving others.

Jesus responded to James and John's request in verse 22 by saying, "you don't know what you ask." Our service suffers when we don't know what it ought to be about, from God's perspective. If our service is about us, making us feel better, making us look better, then it is self-righteous service. Self-righteous service never produces the fruit of the Spirit, the good things we hope for from our lives with Christ. Self-righteous service always disappoints.

The disciples wanted the external reward of exalted positions. They wanted to pick how they would serve Jesus. They, no doubt, felt good about asking for exalted positions before the others could get around to it. They were not sensitive to the whole message Jesus had been communicating. Their request caused a problem in their relationship with the other disciples. The result was that they were not ready for Jesus' response.

His response probably hit them like a ton of bricks. How do I know? Because when Jesus asked them if they were able to drink the cup from which He was about to drink and be baptized with the baptism He was about to be baptized with, they respond, "We are able." What!? "We are able?" Where is their good sense? Where is their humility? They are not able. In fact, they will run with the rest of the disciples when Jesus is arrested. They are not able because they have more to learn about service. They will yet learn the lesson of unselfish service to the glory of God. In verse 23, Jesus predicts that they will indeed learn how to serve and, in so doing, experience the cup He is about to drink and the baptism He is about to endure. But first, they must gain a different perspective on the flesh. This is where failure often proves its unexpected worth.

Too much concern for self makes it hard for us to think about serving. The language of redemption is spoken as we turn our attention totally to others. Redemption will produce in us a capacity to adjust and shake things off and keep going: to persevere. An example of the perseverance that can emerge from a positive response to others and to our circumstances is found in the following story.

A farmer had a donkey who faithfully and unselfishly served him for many years. One day the farmer's donkey fell down into a well. The animal cried for hours as the farmer tried to figure out what to do with the donkey. Finally, he decided the donkey was too old and the well was dried up and needed covering so he would solve the problem by filling in the well with dirt. That way he would not have to dig a grave for the donkey and he would get the old well filled in. He called on his neighbors to come over and help him fill in the well. They all grabbed shovels and began throwing shovels full of dirt into the well. At first when the donkey realized what was happening, he cried out horribly. Then to everyone's amazement the donkey grew very quiet. They kept throwing dirt in and yet there was no sound. Finally, the farmer could stand it no longer. He had to look down into the well and see what was going on. What he saw astonished and amazed him. With every shovelful of dirt that hit his back, the donkey would shake it off and take a step up. He just kept repeating that over and over. He would shake it off and take a step up. Pretty soon to everyone's amazement, the well was filled in and the donkey stepped over the side and happily trotted away.

This donkey was in a situation that had "failure" written all over it. But he responded with something other than discouragement and hopelessness. Your life will be transformed by your unselfish acts of service that exist for the purpose of bringing glory to Jesus Christ. This will leave you with the ability to love unconditionally. Notice that the language of redemption puts a premium on love. This is why loving unconditionally is synonymous with speaking redemption. Like the donkey, I may find myself in a situation that has defeat written all over it. If in those moments I can speak redemption, shake it off, and take a step up, I will unleash a positive momentum that will transform the situation entirely. This is what love looks like: love that is actually strong.

---

## Redemption brings power to heal our hearts.

---

How happy are we to have such a God as God! Yet, at the same time, we cringe at how far our hearts are from the heart of God. We still have a long way to go and, what is more, we still live in the midst of those whose hearts are far from God. In Matthew 15:8 we read, "These people honor me with their lips, but their hearts are far from me." So how do we gain hearts like God's heart? This is an important question, for it will guide our search for the ability to love unconditionally. In Jesus' day, He aimed His strongest teachings and warnings regarding the loss of heart toward the religious people of the day.

Servant-leaders will be under frequent attack, and the target will be our hearts. We know when we are losing heart because our faith will begin to feel more like a series of problems to be resolved and principles to be mastered than a relationship to be enjoyed and a love to be returned.

If our loss of heart is not addressed, our sins and faults will gain a destructive power over us that can crush our spirits and leave us unable to love. Proverbs 4:23 says, "Keep your heart with all diligence, For out of it spring the issues of life."

The people in Isaiah's day faced the challenge of guarding their hearts just as we do today. Because they had not taken care of their hearts, they lost their way. They looked for God's help, His leadership, and His guidance, but something was wrong. The problem was not with God; it was with the people's hearts. The answer to their problem was, and is, confession. Throughout chapter 59 of Isaiah we see, over and over, God pointing to the words coming out of their mouths and the words not coming out of their mouths and how this was affecting their hearts, their relationships with God, and their ability to love:

- "your lips have spoken lies, your tongue has muttered perversity" (v. 3);

- "no one calls for justice . . . they trust in empty words" (v. 4);

- "transgressing and lying against the Lord; speaking oppression and revolt, conceiving and uttering from the heart words of falsehood" (v. 13).

Our words are indicators and instigators of our heart condition. What I mean is that what we hear ourselves say to others and to God says much about our heart condition. It also drives us in a certain direction. If my heart is not healthy, I cannot love and I do not want to love unconditionally.

God's plan is always redemption—to rescue our hearts from the grip of fear and selfishness and guilt. Sometimes when things go wrong, when we experience failure, we can forget that it is God's plan to rescue us. We can even begin to wonder what God is up to and where God is in our storm. This was the case for the Israelites. They were struggling and, in their struggles, they did even greater damage to their hearts through practicing deceit, taking advantage of others, and "[conceiving] evil and [bringing] forth iniquity" (v. 4b). The result was that they could not see God. Their hearts failed and they lost touch with the heart of God. His plan is always rescue. Rescue is the language of redemption. We need to be reminded of God's role in our redemption and the redemption of the people around us. Therefore, Isaiah 59:1 begins by setting the record straight. "Behold the Lord's hand is not shortened, that it cannot save; nor His ear heavy that it cannot hear."

On this occasion, the Israelites were not speaking redemption. Their mouths were filled with every sort of thing other than honesty before the Lord. When we stop being honest with God and with each other about our sins and failures, we lose our connection with God's plan to rescue us. Instead, we start thinking we have to rescue ourselves; this involves trying to keep God in the dark, making Him think we are good, and hiding all our faults from Him and each other. But this approach does not rescue us from trouble; it only hardens our hearts and blinds our eyes to the true source of our rescue. Judgment day is such a scary thought for so many because we rightly suspect that all our posing and posturing, all our pretending and prevaricating, will be exposed. 1 Corinthians 4:5 says the Lord will "expose the motives of men's hearts."

So how do we undo this downward spiral of trying to help ourselves, being frustrated, then forgetting who God is, and in this forgetting causing further struggles? How do we stop the madness? *Speak redemption to yourself and those around you.* Speak of your position as being right in the middle of God's plan of rescue. This reintroduces an element of clarity and perception so longed for and needed. Love reminds me that God's plan is redemption. He knows how to enter the thickest part of my battle and bring me out.

We can fake our way through most things in life and be okay for some time. But something is on the horizon; something is up ahead that you cannot fake your way through. In that moment when your world is shaken to the core, you will need a firm grip on your heart: a heart that is alive and steady and strong in the Lord.

Isaiah 59:2a says, "your iniquities have separated you from your God; your sins have hidden His face from you." You cannot have this separation be the condition of your preparation for facing whatever is next. Verses 3–16 recount in vivid detail what happens to people who face their storms without knowing the language of redemption. The result is devastating!

Too often when we see the storm approaching and we reach down for something deep to hold onto, if we have not practiced speaking redemption, we will find too many doubts and too much uncertainty at the very moment when we need a rock-solid foundation. We need to know the power of God's forgiveness and God's willingness to pay the price for our rescue. This is the rock that steadies us. Yet, if we have spent too much time pretending, we may flounder.

Failure can change the way we approach life's storms, the way we endure life's storms, and the way we emerge from life's storms. To drive this point home, let's consider a storm the disciples found themselves in. In Mark 6, we have the account of Jesus sending the disciples across the Sea of Galilee at night. As they are crossing, a fierce storm erupts. They are terrified, and think they might die! They lose heart. Then Jesus comes to them walking on the water; they think He is a ghost. The power of the storm immediately pales in comparison to the power of Jesus.

We don't sufficiently learn this lesson from hearing someone else talk about how they met Jesus in their storm (though this is helpful). We learn this in our own storms. When we are able to see Christ in the midst of our storm and we see that He is more powerful than our sins and our failure, we gain an ability to speak redemption that is inspirational and life-changing. We must see what is actually happening: Jesus is joining us in the midst of our storm. That means we are worthy! With such affirmation, we are steadied for whatever comes next.

---

## Redemption reminds us of the great provision of God.

---

In the early days of knighthood, a young man was made a knight by his father or liege lord, often on the field of battle. The new knight's sword would be bestowed on the young man and the older man would give him a whack on the shoulder with the flat of the sword. This was called "dubbing" and was the symbolic conferring of the character attributes the knight must live by. Those character attributes were not seen as an additional burden but as the privileges of provision. The knight from thenceforth lived a different life and spoke a different language. Likewise, as Christians, we have been dubbed with the provision of "Christ with us." As we "put on Christ," we live a different life and speak a different language.

Isaiah 59:21b gives us a glimpse into the awesome provision of God for those who are willing to run to Him in times of failure: "'My Spirit who is upon you, and My words which I have put in your mouth, shall not depart from your mouth, nor from the mouth of your descendants, nor from the mouth of your descendants' descendants,' says the Lord, 'from this time and forevermore.'" Did you hear that? Our words of sickness and death are turned into God's words of health and life; our words highlighting our sins and faults are turned into words highlighting the goodness and generosity of God! This is the language of redemption.

How marvelous is the provision of God. It anoints us with the privilege of making a difference not only in our own lives, but in the lives of our children and of our children's children forevermore! Loving unconditionally gives the servant-leader a legacy that keeps on making an impact long after the servant-leader is gone.

---

Redemption brings power to channel our emotions in constructive ways.

---

The language of redemption comes with both the ability to deliver wise counsel and the ability to receive wise counsel. We sometimes misconstrue God's guidance and the God-ordained guidance of those around us, based on how we feel. We so often make leadership too much about us: what we need, what we like, and what we want. Some people are only open to influence and leadership that leads them in the way they wanted to go already.

This approach is dangerous and self-defeating, and is akin to the blind leading the blind. Leadership is most valuable, it seems to me, at the very point where I need to be challenged to do something I don't want to do. God-centered leadership helps me act according to God's will instead of my comfort. The Bible is full of wisdom concerning this learning process:

> *For the time will come when men will not put up with sound doctrine. Instead, to suit their own desires, they will gather around them a great number of teachers to say what their itching ears want to hear.*
> – 2 Tim. 4:3 (NIV)

> *Trust in the LORD with all your heart and lean not on your own understanding.*
> – Prov. 3:5

> *He who trusts in himself is a fool, but he who walks in wisdom is kept safe.*
> – Prov. 28:26 (NIV)

> *Let not the wise man boast of his wisdom or the strong man boast of his strength or the rich man boast of his riches.*
> – Jer. 9:23 (NIV)

A common theme occurs in these verses: whenever learning is only a self-centered matter—"to suit [your] own desires" or "your own understanding" or "trusts in himself" or "boast of [your] wisdom"—it is foolishness.

In Exodus 33:18, Moses makes a bold request of God. We speak a lot of words in our lives, but rarely does anyone articulate words like Moses' words in verse 18. "And he said, 'Please, show me Your glory.'" Moses' love of God and his confidence in God's plan led to his hunger to know and experience God in a deeper and more profound way. Moses knew that the nation of Israel could not meet his need. He knew that just working on his leadership skills would not meet his need. He knew that more money would not meet his need, more friends would not do it, losing weight would not do it, having his candidate win an election would not do it, being respected in his community would not do it, people being impressed by how much he knew his Bible or how religious he was would not do it. The one and only thing that will truly meet all our needs in life is to know our heavenly Father in a deep, profound, experiential relationship. Merely gaining more information about Him, no matter how true and valuable it might be, will ultimately leave us empty.

*Knowledge puffs up, but love builds up.*
– I Cor.8:1b (NIV)

Love builds up. Love builds on the foundation of God's presence. Armorbearers are never content to stand around the edge of God's presence. We are not happy until we are standing in the fire of God's presence! The more we know of God, the more we learn about the God who describes Himself as "God is love," the more we are able to love unconditionally (I John 4:8).

God had started something in Moses' life. God has started something in your life. God's response to Moses' petition included a declaration of His Sovereignty: "I will be gracious to whom I will be gracious, and will show compassion on whom I will show compassion" (Ex. 33:19b). Sovereignty and grace can never be separated. Redemption does not free us from God, it binds us to God. Thus, whenever God's grace is shown, it is done to promote life with God. Sometimes our emotions can run counter to this as we often look to God to give us only what we want with little regard for deeper relationships with Him. But God has started something in your life and it needs to be expressed. It matters not that great obstacles, both inner and outer, must be overcome. Be confident in God's plan.

God has started something in your life. You are going somewhere. Even before you feel good about where you are going as you follow Christ, speak redemption. Don't lower the flag, don't soften the message, don't lose your nerve, and don't get subtle or clever. Don't over-think or underestimate, don't worry. Just remember the unconditional love with which you have been loved, and then love others in the same way.

Moses knew that the best cure for discouragement, disillusionment, and dryness is a fresh glimpse of God. The people had rebelled against the Lord and against Moses' leadership. Can you imagine how Moses must have felt? He has done his best to lead them and to follow the Lord's will, and still all they do is complain and find fault. There must have been many times when Moses wanted to throw in the towel and just quit! But Moses' disappointment did not cause him to withdraw from God; it caused him to seek more of God! Seek more of God and you will love unconditionally; you will speak redemption.

## Redemption empowers us to infuse our serving with celebration.

Let's observe the Master at work. Something interesting happens as Jesus arrives in the village of Bethany where Mary, Martha, and Lazarus live. John 12:1–3 records the moment. "Then, six days before the Passover, Jesus came to Bethany, where Lazarus was who had been dead, whom He had raised from the dead lived. There they made Him a supper; and Martha served, but Lazarus was one of those who sat at the table with Him. Then, Mary took a pound of very costly oil of spikenard, anointed the feet of Jesus, and wiped His feet with her hair. And the house was filled with the fragrance of the oil."

As Christians, we have more reason to celebrate than any people who have ever lived. After what Christ has done for us, we should be experts at joy and optimism. Yet, so many of us struggle with depression when we should be celebrating; we struggle with discouragement when we should be full of hope. Why do we allow ourselves to look at the dark side so much more often than the bright side? Jesus teaches us about celebrating through His interaction with Mary, Martha, Lazarus, Judas, the chief priests, and the crowd.

Verse 2 contains two powerful words: "Martha served." We don't usually equate service with celebration, but we should. Celebration is the dialect of redemption that signals to all that we are from a different place, that a different motivation inspires our service. This is not a call to fake it or go through the motions or act like I am happy when I am not. This is a call to connect with the bigger vision of God for my life and rejoice that I am part of God's plans and purposes. What a privilege we share, of being part of God's great plan of redemption. This truth contains the power to infuse our lives with deep joy.

In the Marines we called this joy "esprit de corps." This is what happens among a group of people who experience shared struggles; it is a bond that deepens their relationships and unleashes a flood of joy and pride. While at Parris Island for Marine training, I was challenged by some fairly serious tests and trials. It wasn't easy, yet I had an interesting experience. Because I was going through this trial with others, a strong bond was formed that changed my attitude. I was able to rejoice in the midst of the training because I so valued the bonds of shared sacrifice. The only time I got into trouble was when I would smile during the training. One might think this an odd response to my suffering. (My drill instructors thought so, and as a consequence added to my training!) I smiled in the middle of hardship because I had a reason to celebrate, and I did celebrate.

People who go through battles together know how to celebrate in ways few others can. This happens when service and obedience are practiced in community. Each person in this story of Jesus' visit to Bethany had an encounter with Christ. We have encounters with Christ through the Word of God, the Spirit of God, and the people of God all the time. But do we lose what is available to us—inspiration to celebrate—because we are too focused on what is required of us? A spirit of celebration is a way of seeing your world; it is a way of responding to your circumstances; it is a way of saying "my God is bigger than my problem, and that deserves to be celebrated!"

Martha decided to serve Jesus and the others. Serving is a fine way of celebrating, if our minds and hearts are right. Martha's serving would not have been celebrating if she was grumbling to herself the whole time, "Mary is so lazy; she should be helping me serve." When we complain as we are doing the right thing, we lose our spirit of celebration and, when we do, we lose something very valuable. Our souls are rallied in the midst of hardships through a spirit of celebration; our attitudes are improved through a spirit of celebration; and our testimony is elevated through a spirit of celebration. Celebrate Christ when you can't say a word, when you have tears in your eyes and hurt in your heart: celebrate because He is with you. Celebrate Christ in your life when your children are difficult or your boss is impossible: celebrate because He is with you. Celebrate Christ when you lose your job or you receive the news, "it's cancer": celebrate because He is with you.

Some will say, "How can I do that; it's not possible?" It is possible when you understand just what is happening. It is all about learning that Christ is more than enough. Can we have a more-than-enough spirit? Martha served. Serving can be celebration if our spirit is right. She may have been uncomfortable expressing herself through words, but she found a way to celebrate her life with Christ. She let her hot biscuits and gravy do the talking for her!

Now we come to Mary and Lazarus. In John 12:3, we see that Mary was pouring expensive perfume on Jesus' feet. She was down at His feet celebrating through the sacrifice of expensive perfume. This was her opportunity and she did not miss it just because it would cost her something! How many opportunities and celebrations have we missed because we thought it would cost us too much? Mary knew that whatever it took to be at the feet of Jesus was worth it. Jesus acknowledged her act. Jesus noticed. That is worth celebrating.

Mary gave away expensive perfume. Lazarus gave away the security that can be found in anonymity. Verses 1 and 2 tell us that Lazarus was present. Verse 9 tells us the people gathered around, not only to see Jesus, but to see Lazarus. All this attention was not a good thing for Lazarus. Verse 10 says the chief priests noticed and "plotted to put Lazarus to death." They were out to get Lazarus. What had he done to them? He was a living, walking billboard, pointing to the power of Jesus. Lazarus knew that hanging around with Jesus publicly would put a target on his back. He could have gone into hiding until everything settled down, but here he was sitting with Jesus. He gave up his privacy and security in order to take advantage of his opportunity to celebrate with Jesus.

Contrast Mary and Lazarus with Judas and the chief priests. Verse 6 tells us that Judas objected to Mary's wasting the perfume, because he controlled the money box. He thought celebrating so lavishly was unnecessary. He missed his opportunity to celebrate Christ, and he lost his life. The chief priests sat around plotting to kill Jesus because they thought He was cutting in on their racket. To them, their power was more important than celebrating Jesus being with them. They lost their opportunity to celebrate Christ and would soon lose their power and their nation.

Your sacrifices, scars, and wounds do not mean you can't celebrate. If you have scars, seize your opportunity and celebrate what Christ has done in your life. If you need to, compare your scars with His and find encouragement.

We dealt first with Martha, then Mary, Lazarus, Judas, and the priests. Now we will deal with the crowd waving the palm branches. Surely they knew how to seize their opportunity and celebrate Jesus. We repeat what they did every Palm Sunday; it's great. Well, not so much. Waving palm branches on Sunday would turn into crying "crucify Him" on the following Friday. Their celebration lacked something important. Their celebration was a result of following the crowd, not a result of taking a stand for Christ. Theirs was no act of conviction; it was more waiting for something to happen, thinking that something, such as Jesus overthrowing the Romans, was about to happen. One of the greatest enemies of celebrating life with Christ is choosing to be passive and following the crowd—instead of being willing to be transformed by Christ no matter the cost and no matter what others might be doing.

Joy and celebration rise out of transformation, not indecision. Don't wait for something to happen. Don't wait until your life is free of failure. Take a stand for Christ. This will usher in a moment, a spirit, a life of celebration. Unconditional love is sometimes expressed with such a dour countenance that the image portrayed is one of defeat or victimization. A spirit of celebration must accompany our expressions of unconditional love so that the strength of being loved is not lost.

Some of my best celebrations take place while fencing with my sons. They are very good fencers. They wield epees with considerable skill. Back when swords were still used as weapons of war or ways to settle disputes, one had to be very skilled in the use of a sword—one's life might depend upon it. One of the hardest things to learn about wielding a sword, then as now, is to be convinced that the sword will work if used properly. The temptation, especially when one is hard-pressed, is to start swinging with all your might in great sweeping motions. Such a handling of the sword is suicide. It leaves you vulnerable to any opponent who knows how to keep his point on target as he keeps his distance.

Love is the language of redemption. I speak this language when I fence with my sons. Our Saturday fencing sessions are not about a display of swordsmanship, they are about communicating the power of redemption. My sons matter to me, and I choose to love them unconditionally. I choose to speak to them the language of redemption. Unconditional love is our overflow. This is how we speak redemption:

> *May the God of hope fill you with all joy and peace as you trust in Him, so that you may overflow with hope by the power of the Holy Spirit.*
> – Rom. 15:13 (NIV)

In this chapter, we have been challenged to practice a love that goes beyond what we can do from places of safety and convenience. We have been exposed to what happens when we love another through looking them in the eyes and saying from our hearts, "Do all that you have in mind. Go ahead; I am with you heart and soul." Yes, it always comes back to the example set by Jonathan's armorbearer. It is much more than simply saying "I love you." Seek to speak redemption. When we do this, all people—not just the people we are attracted to, not just our enemies—will be positively impacted by our ability to speak redemption.

# PART FOUR

# I CHOOSE TO EXERCISE SELF-RESTRAINT

*Wave upon wave, the night grows longer now*
*For a breath, a breeze, my heart calls out*
*Time joins in the negative voices somehow*
*They say stop, say . . . no, they shout*
*Think about yourself, not another*
*Your concerns, your needs, not those of a brother*
*In reply I will not yield, I will not bow*
*Into the fray I have come and will not doubt*
*I cling to His hand now*
*Courage we will not do without*[3]

A great challenge faced by every armorbearer will be the nagging and persistent thought (actually, it may become a negative inner voice that shouts) "look out for yourself before it is too late." If we give in to that voice, we will turn aside from the course of

---

3    Untitled, by Gerald Watford, 2013, all rights reserved.

servant-leadership. Therefore, we must make the crucial choice to practice self-restraint. Without self-restraint, our perspective is always blocked by us. Without self-restraint, our passion is always diverted by excess. Without self-restraint, our potential is always undone by selfishness. By self-restraint I do not mean our working harder to disconnect from anything that causes enjoyment. I mean our commitment to put Christ first and enjoy Him, and live the life that naturally flows from that commitment.

General Nathaniel Greene was assigned the command of the Continental Army in the South during the latter part of the Revolutionary War. He took command at a time when the British forces had just won a series of crushing victories. In fact, American resistance in the Carolinas was thought to be over. With only the defeated remnants of what used to be the American Army in the South, the cause looked hopeless. General Greene adopted a brilliant strategy built on the principle of restraint. His Fabian strategy (named after a famous Roman general who won a seemingly hopeless war this way) meant avoiding the glory of striking a decisive blow. People could not understand this, and so Greene came in for his share of criticism. His was not a popular strategy, but it was a winning strategy. Cornwallis exhausted himself chasing Greene, as Greene restrained his urge to go toe-to-toe with his adversary. Cornwallis eventually abandoned the Carolinas and struck out for Virginia and his date with General Washington—and surrender—at Yorktown.

Self-restraint enables us to better persevere, by directing our energy toward the cause of Christ instead of the distractions of the flesh. In our consumer-driven society, self-restraint has fallen into disfavor, but it is a power waiting to be rediscovered. Someone once said, "A mule cannot kick and pull at the same time; the ones that kick never work." Self-restraint is a call to be powerful in the areas of encouragement and tenacity. These two character traits in fact go hand in hand. The most readily available source of truly powerful encouragement is when we tenaciously stick with another person through life's trials. As armorbearers , we are in the relationship business. In order for God to truly bless us, we must understand that we deal with very sensitive and valuable material. In relationship, you work to gain a position from which you can either do great good or inflict terrible damage. Self-restraint is a commitment to put another before yourself: even over time, even when there is an increasing cost.

We are most likely to find the courage we need when we are surrounded by companions who will not give up on us. Choosing to be an encourager is choosing life in fellowship with others. The fellowship you are invited to be part of has a cross at its center.

---

## Self-restraint is part of the inheritance of the cross.

---

It is Good Friday, the birthday of servant-leadership. A variety of characters have gathered around Jesus. Matthew 27:50–54 records part of the scene:

> And when Jesus had cried out again in a loud voice, he gave up his spirit. At that moment the curtain of the temple was torn in two from top to bottom. The earth shook and the rocks split. The tombs broke open and the bodies of many holy people who had died were raised

to life. They came out of the tombs, and after Jesus' resurrection they went into the holy city and appeared to many people. When the centurion and those with him who were guarding Jesus saw the earthquake and all that had happened, they were terrified, and exclaimed, "Surely he was the Son of God!"

A centurion was the backbone of the Roman army. A centurion was responsible for discipline in the regiment. Each individual centurion had great authority and power because each one had great responsibility. There were times when he not only had to oversee battles, but individual executions, such as the execution of Jesus. Not only in war, but in peace, the centurion was responsible for the morale of the Roman army. The best centurions were also the best encouragers; were those who stuck with their men even in the heat of battle.

In Matthew chapter eight, we read of a centurion who came to Jesus seeking the healing of his servant boy. Jesus says: "I'll come right away to your house and heal the young lad." The centurion said, "No, I'm not worthy that you should even come under my roof; if you only speak the word it will be done. I am a man under authority, and I have men under my authority, and I know when I speak a word one goes and does what I say. I know that if you speak a word, you have the power over disease and death. Jesus, just speak the word."

Armorbearers take responsibility for their choice to be encouragers. This is the fellowship of the cross. We cannot be a part of this fellowship unless we are people who will take personal responsibility for how we impact others. It is so tempting to leave people to reap the consequences of their own choices. Servant-leaders make a different choice.

The centurion had seen many people die in battle. He had been given authority over many executions, but he had never seen a man die like Jesus died. He was given hope through the death of Jesus! When we are serious about being encouragers, when we are serious about developing the capacity to tenaciously impact another's life, God will use even the things we would rather avoid to enable us to make a difference.

Speaking of death, notice that the power unleashed at the cross was encouragement sufficient to cause the dead to rise up out of their graves! Now that is powerful! The power of Christ is a power that clings to us even on the other side of the grave. In the fellowship of the cross, we believe in the power of encouragement and tenacity.

Where do we find the courage we need for the responsibilities we embrace? We need look no further than the example of Christ. The worst thing we can do in order to find courage is to focus on ourself. Self-focus and its offspring, selfishness, creates softness inside us, which leads—not to being courageous and tenacious—but to lack of courage.

---

## Self-restraint gives birth to tenacity, which allows us to cross the point of no return.

---

Tenacity, the child of self-restraint, is the fountain from which encouragement flows. This is the counterintuitive nature of being an armorbearer or servant-leader. Servant-leadership immerses us in a mindset that produces incredible tenacity, which, in turn, equips us to encourage others even in the worst of conditions.

The Battle of Lexington and Concord was the first military engagement of the Revolutionary War. Fought on April 19, 1775, the battle marked the outbreak of armed conflict between England and her American colonies. The first shots were fired when the British troops reached Lexington and encountered the militia formed to block their path. There is a picture that I have from a visit to the site of this battle. This picture is important to me because it represents the point of no return. Tenacity means passing the point of no return and fully committing ourselves to this course in life. There can be no thoughts of turning back allowed in our mind, or turn back we will.

The colonists had been vacillating and hesitating and finding it hard to break their ties to England because, despite all the trouble, being a colony of England was comfortable. So, up until Lexington and Concord, their life had been full of half-measures, backward looks, and tentative steps. After Lexington and Concord, their life was totally different. There would be war. They must fight or die. John Adams put it like this: "the die was cast, the Rubicon crossed." Adams was referring to the crossing of the River Rubicon in Italy by Julius Caesar in 49 BC. In crossing that river, Caesar violated Roman law, a law designed to keep generals and their armies out of Rome, thus preventing military coups. When he crossed the river, it meant war, and thus Caesar said, Alea iacta est: "the die is cast."

Passing the point of no return means taking a course of action with significant and irreversible consequences. Many people struggle with being servant-leaders because they are not willing to live past the point of no return. There is a vast difference in attitude between the person who refuses to pass the point of no return and the person who gladly steps over the line. The difference is the willingness to truly encourage others.

After hearing of the battle at Lexington and Concord, George Washington wrote to a friend, "the once-happy and peaceful plains of America are either to be drenched in blood or inhabited by slaves. Sad alternative! But can a virtuous man hesitate in his choice?" He perceived what Lexington and Concord meant: there was no turning back now.

Being a servant-leader cannot really be done with half measures. Anytime challenges must be faced and overcome, there will be a requirement that we live with a clear understanding of what an irrevocable commitment means.

When he crossed the Rubicon, Julius Caesar had a plan that was sound and farsighted. Caesar quickly advanced to Rome and had himself declared dictator. In a bold, unexpected move, Caesar then led his legions to Spain, where he invited his opponent Pompey's forces to join him and defeated those that would not. After a remarkably short campaign, he returned to Rome and was elected consul, thus legalizing his position. Once you have passed the point of no return, you must have a plan of victory. Without a victory plan, life will quickly become frustrating and fearful. If there is no clear victory plan, people start fighting each other and pulling at cross purposes.

Some of us would rather not know what is going on in other people's lives because it can be unsettling, messy, and intrusive. We prefer nice, safe, comfortable ignorance. But in such a life there is no inspiration to encourage others and no fellowship. There is no esprit de corps in such a life. There is no tenacity that summons the last ounce of resolve from us in such a life. After we have carried our cross for a while, we are able to say with credibility, the cross we carry is never so heavy as the chains from which we were freed. The life of self-restraint opens our eyes to the best that God has to offer us.

- You can never be in so forsaken a place that His love won't seek and find you.

- You can never be so bound in chains that His Spirit can't set your soul free.

- You can never go unrewarded for what you do as a follower of Christ.

Living past the point of no return requires that we encouragers be the most inspired person on the scene. Otherwise our testimony will be confusing. Our worries and fears will send mixed signals about what we truly believe. Our emotions will declare a message that our circumstances are too big for our God.

Credibility is essential for encouragement to work. We can only gain credibility for encouragement through living past the point of no return. So be sure that step over the Rubicon is accompanied with a willingness to take responsibility for being an encourager.

Strange as it sounds, many people are confused about the purpose of their relationship with Christ. Some see it as a religious duty, others a self-help exercise, and others an element of connection to family or societal traditions. All of these things are nice and they are part of a relationship with Christ, but they fall far short if they become the guiding purpose for relating to Christ. Jesus said in Luke 19:10, "for the Son of Man has come to seek and to save that which was lost." This was His purpose, and this must be the purpose of all who follow Him.

---

## Self-restraint is making room for God to work.

---

There are many ways to act on that purpose, as God gives us abilities and opportunities. It is tempting to see a lack of courage in someone and so criticize them. There is another option. When you see a lack of courage in someone, you can take it upon yourself to put courage into them, or be an encourager. This is what Barnabas was to Paul and others. I invite you to meet Barnabas, a master armorbearer. Barnabas made the choice to be an encourager and he stuck to it even when that choice cost him.

Jesus tells a story in Luke 15 in which we see the encouragement gained from one who is tenacious in seeking us and loving us. Verse 4 sets the stage: "What man of you, having a hundred sheep, if he loses one of them, does not leave the ninety-nine in the wilderness, and go after the one which is lost until he finds it?"

Note those last four words—until he finds it. That is tenacity, and it is highly encouraging. The thought that God took the initiative to look for me and pursue me when I was lost is amazing!

The thought that God does not give up on me when I stumble and fall is extremely encouraging.

Jesus didn't give up on others, so neither should we.

Jesus didn't lose heart when confronted with a mess, so neither should we.

Jesus didn't stop involving Himself in the lives of others, so neither should we.

> *Therefore encourage one another and build each other up, just as*
> *in fact you are doing.*
> – I Thes. 5:11 (NIV)

Encouraging others is so important, in fact, that God assumes we will make this one of our top jobs. The epitome of the image of the armorbearer is the encouragement he or she offers as they stand with another person in need, and with an attitude unlike any other. Going back to the story in Luke 15, when the shepherd found the lost sheep, what did he do? Did he say, "This sheep is no good," or did he think "This sheep is not worth my trouble," or did he complain, "This sheep does not even want to be saved?" No, he puts the sheep across his shoulders, and he rejoices! He calls his friends and neighbors together and he celebrates!

We see this bent toward encouragement on another occasion in Scripture when the father sees the prodigal son coming home. The father does not judge or become critical. He restrains any desire to say "I told you so" and he does what must have been most encouraging to the prodigal. The father says, "For this son of mine was dead and is alive again; he was lost and is found." So they began to celebrate (Luke 15:24 NIV). The father restrained his urge to rebuke or berate his son and in so doing maintained his ability to welcome and express love for his son. This is not to say there is never room for discipline or punishment. It is to say that the importance of encouraging another is greater than many understand.

Remember our core passage of Scripture, "Whoever of you desires to be first shall be slave of all. For even the Son of Man did not come to be served, but to serve" (Mark 10:44–45a). To put this into practice, we must first desire to be great (to matter, to make a difference to the glory of God), and then we must make a choice to be a servant. This involves being a slave to all, and then actually serving. Servant-leadership is serving long after others have fallen by the wayside—because you are making room for God to work. The pursuit of greatness is simply that—making room for God to work, because we are convinced that God working is what matters most.

Making the choice to be an encourager is not an invitation to be perpetually emptied and never filled. It is an opportunity to change the basis of your encouraging others from what you can do, to what Christ can do in and through your life. It is making room for God to work.

Jesus was not deterred by either the difficulty of the journey or the potential reticence of the one he found at the end of the journey. This is the encouragement found in tenacity. Jesus set the tone, which many have followed, including a servant-leader named Barnabas.

---

## Self-restraint enables us to not lose our voice amid persecution.

---

Self-restraint gives birth to effective faith expression. When I stop saying everything I want to say, I have greater capacity to say what God would have me say. Hearing yourself say what God would have you say is incredibly more thrilling than hearing yourself say what emanates from your own wisdom.

Christianity was at a low point in Acts 11:19. Stephen had been stoned to death, and a general persecution of all Christians in Jerusalem resulted. But the consequence of all the persecution was that Christians ended up doing what Christ had told them to do in the first place. They scattered, taking the Gospel all over the known world. Before this time of persecution, they had opted for silence and cowering instead of obedience. They remained in Jerusalem, when Christ had told them to preach the Gospel to all people everywhere. The injection of persecution served as the catalyst to get them going. What on the surface looked like (and I am sure to them felt like) a bad thing was, in fact, the thing God used to accomplish His will.

Can you see the good in the midst of the pain? If you can, then you must declare it, because it will make a difference in the lives of others. If you want to be an encourager, you must be able to have vision enough to see that persecution or pain or hardships produce positive results when God's people are serving and trusting Him.

Many people lose their vision and their voice when difficulty or persecution strikes. Therefore, most of us lose our ability to be encouragers in hard times, but these are the times when people need encouragement the most. When we cannot understand, we usually end up pointing fingers, complaining, and criticizing each other. When we can find nothing positive, we run with the negative.

In Genesis 50:20, Joseph makes a comment that can only come from the mouth of one who has learned the value of tenacity in the face of adversity and has benefited from being encouraged and is now encouraging. "You intended to harm me, but God intended it for good to accomplish what is now being done, the saving of many lives." (NIV)

Joseph lived to see a huge negative in his life turned into an even bigger positive, because he embraced the life of a servant-leader. When we do what God commands, the hand of the Lord is with us and the result is always good. When you know this, you have something positive and encouraging to say.

Acts 11:21 provides the conclusion of what happens when people trust the Lord even in the presence of persecution: "and the hand of the Lord was with them, and a great number believed and turned to the Lord." An encourager is the person who can see something of what God is up to in the midst of the mess, and who can then share that message with others.

Servant-leaders know how to nudge others in the right direction when action is required. In 1775, Patrick Henry spoke these words at St. John's Church in Richmond, Virginia:

Sir, we have done everything that could be done to avert the storm which is now coming on. . . . we have prostrated ourselves before the throne. . . . Our petitions have been slighted . . . our supplications have been disregarded. . . . If we wish to be free—If we mean to preserve inviolate those inestimable privileges for which we have so long been contending . . . we must fight! I repeat it, sir, we must fight! An appeal to arms and to the God of hosts is all that is left us! They tell us, sir, we are weak, unable to cope with so formidable an adversary. But when shall we be stronger? Will it be next week, or next year . . . shall we gather strength by irresolution and inaction. . . . Sir, we are not weak if we make a proper use of those means which the God of nature hath placed in our power. . . . Besides, sir, we shall not fight our battles alone. There is a just God who presides over the destinies of nations . . . The battle, sir, is not to the strong alone; it is to the vigilant, the active, the brave. . . . The war is inevitable—and let it come! I repeat it sir, let it come. . . . Gentlemen may cry "peace, peace"—but there is no peace. The war is actually begun! The next gale that sweeps from the North will bring to our ears the clash of resounding arms! Our brethren are already in the field! Why stand we here idle? What is it that gentlemen wish? What would they have? Is life so dear, or is peace so sweet, as to be purchased at the price of chains and slavery? Forbid it, Almighty God! I know not what course others may take; but as for me, give me liberty or give me death!

Those are the words of a man who has not lost his voice. As we saw in the life of Jonathan's armorbearer, in Peter's life, in

David's life, and in Barnabas' life, armorbearers do not lose their voice in difficult times.

---

## Self-restraint informs us of our own resilience.

---

Self-restraint results in amazing resilience. When we practice resilience, we will inspire those around us.

The church in Jerusalem was resilient. When they heard of what was going on in other churches, they sent Barnabas to encourage these other believers. Remember, this was a church undergoing persecution. Shouldn't they have been hunkered down, moaning and complaining about their hardships? So many times we circle the wagons and go into a defensive posture at the very moment we should be going on the offensive. What an inspiration and encouragement this little, beat-up, persecuted church in Jerusalem became for other churches. They exhibited resilience. Resilience is the ability to recover readily from illness, depression, and adversity. It is a close relative of tenacity. It is not what happens to us, but how we respond to what happens to us that is a variable we can control.

People have long tapped into resilience to inspire others. Consider an example from America's founding. Sgt. William Jasper was serving with the 2nd South Carolina Regiment on June 28, 1776, when the British attacked Ft. Sullivan (now called Ft. Moultrie). The flag flying over the fort was shot down and fell to the bottom of the ditch on the outside of the fort. Sgt. Jasper saw this and leaped into the ditch, exposing himself to enemy cannon fire. Jasper recovered the flag, tied it to a piece of wood lying nearby, and placed it back on the fort's parapet. Then he stayed in this exposed position supporting the flag until a permanent flag staff could be procured and fixed in place. Jasper's actions demonstrated resilience in the face of great danger, and this rallied his fellow soldiers, who then kept up their resistance until sunset. In the face of this resilience, the British retreated and did not succeed in taking Charleston for another five years. Sgt. Jasper was an armorbearer whose actions inspired Americans all across the colonies and throughout the long war that followed.

In my police training, we had a class in which we heard eyewitness testimony about two different shooting incidents involving police officers. One officer was shot and thought he was fatally wounded. He stopped fighting and was eventually killed, even though his initial wound was not that serious. Another police officer was seriously wounded but refused to believe it was enough to keep him down, so he kept fighting until the criminal was stopped.

You were created by God, you are made of tougher stuff than you give yourself credit for, and it is important to dig down deep in moments of trial and find a way to get up. Like I tell my sons: "You can do more than you think you can!"

When we practice resilience, we inspire those around us. The church in Jerusalem was resilient. When they heard of what is going on in other churches, they sent Barnabas to encourage these other believers. They did not say to themselves what many others might have: "Hey, they should be sending someone to encourage us!" Acts 11:23 tells us that Barnabas was glad when he heard what was going on and he encouraged them, and verse 24 gives us an insight into his attitude: "for he was a good man, full of the Holy Spirit and of faith, and a great many people were added to the Lord."

Notice that we do not get a lot of detail about what Barnabas said to encourage them. It was not so much about what he said as it was who he was and what he represented. He was a member of a persecuted church reaching out to encourage others. He was a good man whose life was open to the leading of the Holy Spirit. He was a servant-leader whose tenacity and resilience were inspiring. This is what an encourager looks like. Understand your own resilience and you will be far advanced down the road of being an encourager.

Robert Whiting, an elderly gentleman of 83, arrived in Paris by plane. At the French immigration control desk, he took a few minutes to locate his passport in his carry on. "You have been to France before, monsieur?" the customs officer asked sarcastically. Mr. Whiting admitted that he had been to France previously. "Then you should know enough to have your passport ready." The American said, "The last time I was here, I didn't have to show it." "Impossible! Americans always have to show their passports on arrival in France!" The American senior citizen gave the Frenchman a long, hard look. Then he quietly explained, "Well, when I came ashore at Omaha Beach on D-Day in 1944 to help liberate this country, I couldn't find a single Frenchman to show my passport to."

Who is more of a Frenchman, the man who takes for granted all the blessings of freedom in France, or the man who was willing to tenaciously lay down his life on the field of battle so that France could be freed from tyranny? When we become absorbed with lives of ease and begin to disdain sacrifice, we lose touch with our resilience.

Do not develop an appetite for the fake instead of the genuine article. We can go through seasons of our lives where we miss seeing the most important thing, even when it is right under our noses. Many of us can look back on long years of our lives when we missed what was most important because we focused too much on ourselves.

Servant-leaders like Barnabas are drawn to what is real. You can get by on substitutes for a while, but at some point the result will be devastating. The most devastating thing about substitutes is that they never lead to greatness.

Pat is a lady at church who is an armorbearer and who has mastered being an encourager. Her spirit so overflows with the positive vibes of an encourager that you cannot help but get some of it on you when in her presence. She has so made the choice to be an encourager that it has shaped her character. She has become resilient, and she does something so special: she sees value in others.

---

Self-restraint enables us to deepen our level of commitment to others, even at great expense to ourselves.

---

Acts 11:25 says, "Barnabas departed for Tarsus to seek Saul." This sounds like a minor incident, but let's consider. Tarsus is about eighty-six miles from Antioch. That is quite a distance to walk. In those days, travel was dangerous due to a number of factors: highwaymen, animals, lack of food, weather. So Barnabas not only goes to Antioch, he leaves to get Paul and then walks back with Paul. He and Paul spend an entire year teaching the people. This qualifies as going above and beyond. This is a level of commitment that is highly encouraging.

To pay the cost of deep investment in others, we must tap into an additional character quality that is produced by self-restraint. Self-restraint gives birth to sight-enhancing impartiality. When we practice self-restraint, we see other people's lives with an impartiality that reveals to us a plan of action.

My wife and I have been married over twenty-six years, and she is powerful in my life because she sees value in me. She knows me perhaps better than any other person, and still she sees value in me as a person. This may sound like a small thing, but it is huge. We live in a world in which so many people are told that they don't matter, that they are not valuable.

One of the greatest things we can do is make a positive impact on others, but this is such a rare thing because most of us try to make an impact while maintaining a comfortable distance. We want the benefit of a positive impact but also a quick getaway. But this is how we lose our impact. We can't have both.

---

## Self-restraint enables us to reap the benefits of tenacity.

---

Self-restraint not only gives birth to tenacity; it enables us to reap the benefits of tenacity. In the Bible, a woman named Ruth had the quality of tenacity (see Ruth 1:16–18). Her life left an impact reaching through the centuries. Ruth can teach us how to make a better impact. Ruth's impact as a servant-leader occurred in the face of enormous obstacles, but these obstacles simply served to set the stage for her success. Ruth was from Moab, a region adjacent to Israel, just over the Jordan River. The Moabites were despised by the Israelites. So Ruth's example of tenacity took place under the following conditions:

- Ruth was from a despised people;

- she was only an in-law, not a blood relative;

- she was an in-law in a family that had just lost the bread-winner;

- she was an in-law in a family that was poor, and with no prospects;

- she was an in-law in a family headed back to Israel, where she could expect nothing but abuse;

- she was an in-law taking a lonely stand, as her sister-in law turned back for home.

Naomi told her two daughters-in-law that they should stay behind in their own land. Orpah took her up on the offer. What is strange is that Ruth did not. Ruth 1:14 tells us she clave, which means "to cling, adhere, to stick to." Remember, stickiness cannot take place from a distance. It is not a detached, uninvolved activity. It is joining oneself to another or to a belief, and refusing to let go. We tend to lose our stickiness when we focus on all the circumstances that are not in our favor. But God invites us to see unfavorable circumstances in a different light. Ruth teaches us that we can be sticky, a person of impact, a servant-leader, even if we are surrounded by:

- people who come from a different race;

- people who come from a broken home, or where death or pain are evident;

- people who are down on their luck;

- people who have made mistakes;

- people who are without prospects.

Naomi was all of these things, and yet Ruth clung to her with a deep love and commitment, which, no doubt, made an unforgettable and indelible impact on everyone around. Ruth was not distracted or deterred by what people might think, what it might cost her (she was after all, an eligible widow who could quickly remarry if she stayed in her own land), or whether or not Naomi could ever do anything for her in return. An elderly widow was at the bottom of that society, someone with nothing to offer but begging. Ruth's ability to be an armorbearer came from her sticking to a set of values and being infused with God's sense of impartiality.

God's impartiality is hard for many people to grasp. We tend to be such partial people. We like certain qualities in a person. We tend to be receptive to particular characteristics and a certain look. We are partial to certain personalities and people more than others. We like what we like and frown upon what we don't like.

Having a natural affinity for certain kinds of people and a natural dislike for others is not the problem. The problem arises when we refuse to see the value of every person.

Romans 2:11 says, "For God does not show favoritism." (NIV)

Acts 10:34–35 says, "Then Peter began to speak: 'I now realize how true it is that God does not show favoritism, but accepts men from every nation who fear him and do what is right..'" (NIV)

God chose Ruth, a woman whose background was less than ideal (according to the Jews), to pour out His love and blessings upon. He brought her into contact with Boaz and He blessed her life exceedingly. She became part of the lineage of Jesus Christ. Speaking of Christ, He demonstrated an impartial love to the whole world. He is impartial in His love and His offer of salvation to all who would come by faith, regardless of color, creed, or background. No one is disqualified because they don't have enough money or don't have the right clothes. Our attitudes as servant-leaders must be formed by the example and the teachings of Christ.

William Wilberforce faced endless discouragement in his battle against the slave trade in England. He was in great need of encouragement one night when he opened his Bible and a small piece of paper fell out. It was a letter written by John Wesley to him: "Unless the divine power has raised you up . . . I see not how you can go through your glorious enterprise in opposing that [abominable practice of slavery], which is the scandal of religion, of England, and of human nature. Unless God has raised you up for this very thing, you will be worn out by the opposition of men and devils. But if God be for you, who can be against you? Are all of them together stronger than God? Oh, be not weary of well-doing. Go on in the name of God, and in the power of His might."

Wilberforce invested twenty-six years of intense effort and, shortly before his death in 1833, England abolished the slave trade. Wilberforce's tenacious commitment to those who were different from him, those who could do nothing for him, was the vehicle God used to lead England in freeing her slaves.

Have you sent the message to others that you will cling to them, you will be there for them, that you are fastened tightly to them so that their welfare is your welfare, their hardships are your hardships, their tears are your tears?

Barnabas sacrificed greatly for the believers in Antioch. Seeing true value in others is the great quality a world-class encourager possesses. This is why my wife is such a great encouragement to me. Do you have someone in your life who has made significant sacrifices for you?

---

## Self-restraint equips us to make a difference in the lives of our enemies.

---

There is an even greater arena available for those who wish to excel in encouraging and tenacity. Seeing value in our enemies and encouraging them is a frequently overlooked opportunity available to us all. Those who venture here are truly great indeed.

Abraham Lincoln was an amazing servant-leader because he saw value in the whole nation: not just the North but the South as well. He left a legacy so encouraging to us as a nation, and we honor him as one of America's greatest presidents because he saw value in all people.

Lincoln let go of so much that is normal among enemies, and he sacrificed his life so that America might be given, in his words, "a new birth of freedom." Abraham Lincoln let go of hatred and revenge and instead chose to be generous and kind. At a time when America was a nation bitterly divided by people whose hatred overflowed, Lincoln's words reflect someone who was able to see value in others: "With malice toward none, with charity for all; with firmness in the right, as God gives us to see the right, let us strive on to finish the work we are in, to bind up the nation's wounds."

Lincoln sacrificed any satisfaction to be had from exacting revenge or celebrating over the demise of his adversary, because he saw value in others. He celebrated the "binding up of the nation's wounds." He gave up so much so that he could accomplish the greater goal and the greater good of bringing people back together.

We often hear the call today, "Why can't we all just get along?" "Why can't the Republicans and Democrats work together?" It is because no one wants to see and proclaim the value in those they disagree with and then act on that understanding. We become irresistible encouragers when we spend time uncovering the value in others, especially those for whom there is some built-in animosity.

Shadows of discouragement stretch over many lives, and too many people are content with living in those shadows. If I am going to stop living in the shadows, I have to understand what causes the shadows in my life. Somewhere along the way, we can lose touch with the pervasive, eroding, and wearying nature of conflict. People in the midst of conflict need a lot of extra encouragement, and many people spend far too much time in this conflict with far too little encouragement. I heard a fine example of encouragement recently. Two little children are in a hospital, lying on beds next to each other, waiting outside the operating room. The first child leans over and asks, 'What are you in for?" The second child says, "I'm in here to get my tonsils out, and I'm a little nervous." The first child says, "You've got nothing to worry about. I had that done when I was four. They put you to sleep, and when you wake up, they give you lots of jello and ice cream. It's a breeze." The second child asks, "What are you in here for?" The first child says, "A circumcision." And the second child says, "Whoa, good luck with that one, buddy! I had that done when I was born . . . I couldn't walk for a year!"

It all starts when we get hurt. We don't understand how or why it happened, so we begin struggling to make sense of things. Was it because someone betrayed me, or was it because God did not do what He could have done? Most people get stuck at some point because God appears to be up to something other than what we expected. At this point, we can get really complicated in our approach to life and end up asking a lot of "why?" questions. A feeling that we are unloved can create long shadows. But as the battle rages, for us to ask "why is God silent?" is like being on a battlefield caught in a crossfire and asking, "God, why are they shooting at me?" We live in the midst of conflict but the good news is we can, even so, live life to its fullest. To do this, it is important that we not try to respond to our troubles by coming up with our own solutions. Like when we try to surround ourselves with stuff to find some level of joy as a solution to pain and disappointment, all we do is add a layer of complexity that puts us in the dark. Or when we want to be loved, but we act in ways that make it hard for others to love us.

You are valuable! Don't let the long shadows fool you. What do you do when things don't work like they are supposed to? Maybe it is a marriage or a job; maybe it is a fishing net like Peter's, which would not work like it was supposed to even after being cast out all night long. How many times have we quietly thought to ourselves, "This is not what I hoped for. This is not what I expected. O God, what is going on? I need for you to heal the one I love, to repair the breach I caused. Yet it seems that you are up to something different from what I expected."

---

## Self-restraint will deliver us to the middle of our best dreams.

---

What dream are you about to let go of? Trials will inevitably leave us feeling a little deflated. But know that God has never stopped working on your behalf. God remains actively involved, working in ways you can't always see, to bring you to that moment when your boat is so full you have to call for help in handling the abundant blessings. Be encouraged. It has been those petitions offered up in the hard times, in moments where there seemed to be no hope, that God has heard and responded to. He has a simple command to you: get back up!

- Go back out there one more time. Get back up!

- This problem is not bigger than your God. Get back up!

- You matter to God. Get back up!

- You matter to someone whom God has raised up and who is headed your way. Get back up!

- There is an armorbearer coming, someone who God has equipped to encourage you. Get back up!

If we are going to make the choice to be encouragers, we must see life differently. This mess is not that dream God told you about. Maybe the mess is a bad relationship, financial hardship, health problems, or problems at work. Just because your life is temporarily a mess, does that mean you can't live for Christ? No! Don't live the mess, live the dream.

There is a beautiful story toward the end of Joseph's life, where he is unveiled before his brothers. Joseph's brothers think he was probably dead long ago, or at best he has become some broken-down slave. But Joseph never stopped living the dream of who he was: the servant of the living God. The brothers are living their mess. They find themselves standing before what they think is an angry Egyptian lord, equal in power to Pharaoh himself. Their knees are knocking. Finally, unable to hold back his tears of joy, Joseph reveals himself to his brothers. Joseph's glory was evident because he never gave up on the dream God told him about when he was a little boy.

The real Peter is unveiled at Pentecost when he preaches a sermon and 3000 people are converted. The real Peter was not the man who denied Jesus. That was just a mess that happened. Peter never gave up on the dream that God told him about when he said, "upon this rock I will build my church."

Moses put a veil over his face because he struggled with the dream God told him. We do that, too. We cover our glory or we let someone cover it for us. But we were called to shine!

Zechariah 9:16–17a says, "The Lord their God will save them on that day as the flock of his people. They will sparkle like jewels in a crown. How attractive and beautiful they will be!" (NIV)

Matthew 5:16 says, "Let your light shine before men." (NIV)

Philippians 2:15 and 16 includes, "You shine like stars in the universe as you hold out the word of life."

This place of difficulty you are in is not that place God told you about. Jesus says in John 14:2b–3, "In My Father's house are many mansions; if it were not so, I would have told you. I go to prepare a place for you. And if I go and prepare a place for you, I will come again and receive you to Myself; that where I am, there you may be also." So, why do we act as if this place is more important than that place? This place is not that place. We are a royal priesthood, a people from a prepared place. When we get confused about where we are from, we get confused about who we are. God tells us in Romans 8:30b, "Those He justified, He also glorified" (NIV). When we don't feel glorified, we don't act glorified. We act like we are from this place where they teach you Christianity is about being nice and trying not to sin. If you really want to know who you are, look at the place God is preparing for you. God is not preparing a place for sin. He is preparing a place for you. Don't let your current place dictate who you are, how you will live, and how you will act.

Misunderstanding is a great danger we face when walking by faith. It is understandable that others sometimes misunderstand you, but don't you misunderstand who you are, what you are about, and where you are from as a servant-leader.

So many people misunderstand God. They deal with God as if He were a father they never liked, or an ex-spouse. So many of us deal with God's commands as if they were meant to harm us or rob us of our freedom or make life difficult for us. That is what the world teaches, but that is not what God teaches. This God is not that god the world has told you about. This God of the Bible is not that god of the world. This God gives you glory; He makes you holy. Why would we hold ourselves at a distance from such a God?

Whatever difficult circumstance you might be facing right now, remember it has passed through the hands of God. So don't respond to this circumstance as if God somehow let it slip by Him. Don't respond to this event in your life, which God has equipped you for, as if it were that event in your life you tried to face without God. This is not that circumstance. This day is not that day when we walked in disobedience. This day is not that day when we tried to protect our own glory while we ignored God's glory. This is the day that God has made, and you are the person to whom God has given His glory.

"The World Turned Upside Down" is an English Ballad. It was first published in 1643 as a protest against Oliver Cromwell's outlawing of traditional English Christmas celebrations. When Lord Cornwallis surrendered the British army at the Siege of Yorktown in 1781, the British band played this tune as they walked out to surrender to the American army under General Washington. Their world had been totally disrupted in a radically unexpected way. This was something big, something they could not ignore. When facing big things, we must believe that they have passed through God's hands or we will lose our ability to encourage others. Indeed, we will lose our ability to keep our own optimism intact.

Remember who you are. Trevor Horn and Gavin Greenaway remind us with these words:

> *Then from on high—somewhere in the distance*
> *There's a voice that calls—remember who you are*
> *If you lose yourself—your courage soon will follow*
> *So be strong tonight—remember who you are.*[4]

Self-restraint is the key to developing the kind of memory that points us to our real strength, our real glory, our real tenacity, and our real identity in Christ. When this reminder is in place, we are free to encourage others through making a deeper investment in their lives.

As we have seen, to make a deeper investment in the lives of others we must become impartial. Otherwise, we will turn back before the job is finished. Too many of us turn back before we arrive at the point where we can make our fullest impact. If we

---

4    Trevor Horn and Gavin Greenaway, "Sound the Bugle," recorded by Bryan Adams on Spirit: Stallion Of The Cimarron, 2002, A&M Records, http://bryanadams.com/index.php?target=archive,official_releases&view_releases=list&show_release=23, accessed on Nov. 20, 2013.

want to encourage, that opportunity only lies beyond some sacrifice, some price of time or emotional investment.

We must battle our bent toward individualism. Yes, each person is responsible for his or her choices, but we are also responsible for our impact or lack thereof. It is easy to see a mess and say "Wow, I am glad that was not me." But encouragement comes when we respond differently: "Your mess is my mess. I am not looking for you to have your act together. I am looking for you to embrace a friend, to see life as a shared endeavor." Deception will lead us to say, "I have enough problems; I don't need any more." This deception leads to thinking that our best approach to problem-solving will be to focus on ourselves. This is deception. When you tackle things alone, hard and far will be your fall. But the small amount of time and energy it takes to be involved in other people's lives will unleash a different spirit in your own life. This different spirit, of being a part of something bigger than yourself, of being united to others in a shared struggle, makes your problems shrink and makes God's provision clear.

In this section we have seen the power available to those who take seriously the choice of being a tenacious encourager. Our journey has taken us from considerations of what we personally give up and put at risk, to considerations of how to love those around us, to how to make a positive impact on every life, even those who may at one level irritate us or violate some notion of beauty or propriety we may have. Encouragement is the fine point, the sharpened tip of the sword, of servant-leadership. It is being able to say, when it is most difficult to say, "Do all that you have in mind. Go ahead; I am with you heart and soul."

# CONCLUSION

MY GOAL HAS NOT BEEN to teach so much as it has been to expose you to what is best caught. The outline of servant-leadership can be defined and taught, but the essence of servant-leadership is a vision that has to be caught. I believe we can all catch—from God and from the examples of armorbearers like the ones you have met—the ability to make a positive impact when it matters most. This is the great opportunity of our lives. My favorite poem captures so well our encounters with opportunity.

### Opportunity
### By Edward Rowland Sill

*This I beheld, or dreamed it in a dream:—*
*There spread a cloud of dust along a plain;*
*And underneath the cloud, or in it, raged*
*A furious battle, and men yelled, and swords*
*Shocked upon swords and shields. A prince's banner*
*Wavered, then staggered backward, hemmed by foes.*
*A craven hung along the battle's edge,*
*And thought, "Had I a sword of keener steel—*

*That blue blade that the king's son bears,—but this*
*Blunt thing—!" He snapped and flung it from his hand,*
*And lowering crept away and left the field.*
*Then came the king's son, wounded, sore bested,*
*And weaponless, and saw the broken sword,*
*Hilt-buried in the dry and trodden sand,*
*And ran and snatched it, and with battle-shout*
*Lifted afresh he hewed his enemy down,*
*And saved a great cause that heroic day.*[5]

A great opportunity has arrived. Yes, it will sometimes seem like an invitation to pick up a broken sword. Well, pick up your broken sword, swing it with all your might, and celebrate your victory! You have been prepared just as God has always prepared His people.

To learn God's view of our difficulties, read Jeremiah 12:5.

If you have run with the footmen, and they have wearied you, then how can you contend with horses? And if in the land of peace, in which you trusted, they wearied you, then how will you do in the floodplain of the Jordan?

In Jeremiah's day, the Jordan River was a formidable obstacle to entering the Promised Land. Not only were there no bridges, but the river was prone to rising suddenly, and enemies abounded in the area who knew well how to take advantage of someone in the vulnerable position of crossing a river. On top of

5 Edward Rowland Sill, as quoted on the All Poetry website, accessed on Nov. 19, 2013, http://allpoetry.com/poem/8543567-Opportunity-by-Edward_Rowland_Sill.

all that, in those days wild animals frequented the river banks. So crossing the Jordan was a significant undertaking, requiring close planning and full of lessons to be learned. Remembering that it is God's will to work through His servants, we learn from Jeremiah 12:1–5:

- God never sends a person into the wilds of the Jordan without training him in a land of relative peace.

- God never sends a person to run with horses until he has first practiced with the footmen.

Through what we encounter today, God is equipping us for what we will face tomorrow. He is equipping us with a response different and better than the way the world responds, so we need hold no affection for copying the ways of the world. How well we do close to home, where everything is conducive for our encountering, fully, the Word of God, will set the tone for how well we do as we move out into the world. If a person stumbles close to home, how will he fare later in hostile territory? "Jeremiah," God is saying, "if you think this is bad, how will you cope when it really gets tough? And it will get tougher."

Here is what *tougher* is for most of us: God does not give us permission to just cross the Jordan and forget about everyone left on the other side (see Matt. 28:19). Here is *tough*: leaving the safety of where you are and going back to help another. What we do when God calls us to recross the river to seek those on the other side reveals the true nature of our leadership and character.

- Why didn't Jeremiah quit and tell God it was hopeless?

- What kept Moses going through long years in the wilderness?

- What kept David deeply in love with God?

- What caused Paul to endure all kinds of hardships and come away rejoicing?

- What motivated Jonathan's armorbearer to respond as he did in the face of such overwhelming odds?

They got it! They had learned that God has a better way, a better response for us than copying the way the world does things. God's way is to use even broken vessels like us for His work, for His glory. Isn't that amazing?! God is training us so that we can be His representatives on this Earth, so that we can learn and live and love even in the midst of all the pain and frustration. On His training ground, we learn how to be servant-leaders, so that we will know what to do when our time comes to cross the river.

Servant-leadership is accepting Jesus' redefinition of greatness. It is using my position not to make much of me but to serve others and, in so doing, to follow the example of Christ and bring Him glory. Yes, He calls us to do things that we don't normally see strong and powerful people do, but He is not calling us to be weak or victims. He is calling us to serve. He is calling us to access the great treasure of being "more than conquerors."

Every encounter with Jesus leads to a place of service.

Jesus calls His disciples to be fishers of men. We can't do this without serving others.

Jesus calls His disciples to wash other peoples' feet. We can't do this without serving others.

Jesus sends forth His disciples under such teachings as forgive, turn the other cheek, love your enemy. We can't do those things without serving others.

Jesus sends us forth into the storms and messes of life: things that we would rather avoid. We want to avoid the mess, but Jesus reminds us that it is for such a time as this that we are made. He is not rescuing us from the mess. He is equipping us to be victorious in the mess, to keep serving in and through the mess, and in so doing, to be rooted deeper in a more confident and bold faith so that we can make a difference. Servant-leaders are those who go through life not seeking to be made much of but seeking to serve others, to love others unselfishly to the glory of God.

Galatians 6:14a says, "May I never boast except in the cross of our Lord Jesus Christ" (NIV). No small thing, this, but once we set out to take hold of the life built upon such a foundation, we will encounter the power and love of God as we never could otherwise.

---

We cannot overcome what is before us if we are unsure of what is inside of us.

---

The great Scottish Presbyterian minister, Robert Murray McCheyne, who learned much about servant-leadership in his short life, wrote this:

> Remember you are God's sword—His instrument—I trust, a chosen vessel unto Him to bear His name. In great measure, according to the purity and perfections of the instrument will be the success.

We have taken a journey. What a journey it has been! We have had many encounters with both the darker portions of our nature and the brighter light we can be through making the choices of servant-leadership. We have become acquainted with the rich inheritance we share from God and, as a result, we have been confronted with the question, "Now, what are you going to do?" To respond as servant-leaders, we must always remember the abundance of our blessings, because generosity will always be a vital part of the instigation for our actions.

> *A generous man will prosper; he who refreshes others will himself be refreshed.*
> – Prov. 11:25 (NIV)

It is that essential element of being revived, refreshed, and renewed as we go through life that means so much. But do not simply opt for the path of duty or increased effort: these will leave you discouraged and weary. Being a successful servant-leader depends on having your own soul perpetually refreshed.

And servant-leadership depends on passion: passion, not emotion. Passion includes emotion, but emotion does not always include passion. This entire journey has been about passion: passion for God and for living as God would have us live. Emotions change; they fade. Passion emerges like a rock, slow to arrive but, once in place, it has the permanence of a mountain. Emotions have their greatest impact on the individual expressing them. Passion has its greatest impact not only on the individual marked by it, but on those who are in its path. Most people do not have to work hard to find emotions. However, many people search all their lives and never find their passion. Emotions are all about how I feel. Passion is all about how I am willing to live, given the vision I have caught. Passion is invaluable. It not only changes lives, it changes the world.

So where do we find our passion? It is not in looking at how we feel or what we want or what we like. It is in discovering that life was meant for bigger things than just me looking out for me. Passion is uncovered when I am willing to let go of me and take hold of the difference I can make for the glory of God.

In India, there are a lot of monkeys and often they become pests, eating food and even attacking children. When the locals want to catch one, they anchor a bottle in a place the monkeys frequent; the neck of the bottle is just large enough for a monkey's hand to fit through. Then, they put a small banana in the bottle, sit back, and wait.

Before long a monkey comes by, sees the banana, reaches his hand into the bottle, and grabs it. Then the monkey discovers that he can't get his hand out of the bottle while holding onto the banana. The monkey could, of course, let go of the banana and run away before getting caught. But he doesn't, because the banana has value to the monkey and the monkey is unwilling to let go of it, even at the cost of his freedom.

As Christians, we can find ourselves in a similar situation. We can hold onto something that has some value to us, even though it may cost us our freedom and power in Christ. To take hold of the life of an armorbearer, we must be willing to let go of other priorities: priorities that may have value, but that detract us from positioning ourselves to serve.

Perhaps the hardest thing about letting go is that it so often feels like failure. In Genesis 43:1–14 we have the story of Joseph's brothers coming to him in Egypt for food. The brothers don't know it is Joseph, but Joseph knows them. As they prepare to return home, Joseph instructs them that if they come back, they must be sure to bring their youngest brother, Benjamin. This means Israel the father will have to let go of his son Benjamin. From this situation we can learn much about letting go, so that we might take hold of an armorbearer's life.

---

## We must look again at what we are so afraid of, and rethink how to proceed.

---

Verse 1 tells us that there was a severe famine in the land of Israel. So the people had a great need: food. But for Israel that need was laden with fear—the fear of losing his youngest son as he had already lost his favorite son, Joseph.

As people of faith, we have committed ourselves, just as the Israelites did, to a certain course of action: that we will walk by faith in the Lord our God. Now to get what we need, we cannot stop walking by faith. And fear causes us to stop walking by faith. This is how we get ourselves into trouble. This is how we become monkeys holding onto the banana in the jar even though we know it will cost us our freedom and our purpose.

As people of faith, we must be willing to trust God even when it seems as if God is calling us to make too great a sacrifice. Israel wanted food, but in order to get food, he had to let go of Benjamin. Israel had lost Joseph, so he clung fiercely to Benjamin. Benjamin represented Israel's security; he was acting as if something other than God was the source of his security. He was acting as if his security was more important than his God. What is God's role in our security? Jesus tells us: "But seek first His kingdom and His righteousness, and all these things will be given to you as well" (Matt. 6:33 NIV).

What is the best way to keep a ship safe, to make sure it does not sink? Keep it in port, and preferably in dry dock. But to do so is to rob a ship of its purpose. For faith to work, there must be the presence of the unknown. The presence of the unknown makes us afraid, granted. But we must not allow our fear to be the deciding factor. Look again at what you are so afraid of and ask yourself: is God bigger than that?

---

## We must be open to redefining success and reconsidering what it means to be human.

---

To return to our story: Israel's entire perspective is shaped by his belief that his sons have failed him and dealt wickedly toward him by telling the Egyptian leader (Joseph) that there is another brother back at home. He is allowing no other option than the thought that this is a disaster. He sees his precious son going to Egypt and being lost forever. That's because, to him, success means Benjamin being at his side always. But God is challenging Israel to drop his banana. He will challenge each of us to redefine success and to drop the world's definition.

What does it mean to be human? Is it not to love God and others more than I love myself? Is not love the defining characteristic of humanity, and is not love the call to put another before myself? Philippians 2:3 instructs us to be humble and think of others as better than ourselves. Being self-centered is a perversion of our humanity. Real success is me making the choice to live closer to God and to trust Him with the consequences.

The life of an armorbearer is living a life as close as possible to the ideal of what it means to truly be human—which is having a Christlike character—until we see Christ face to face. Such a life takes incredible strength of character. Have you seen those athletes who are so accomplished that they make even the most difficult athletic feats look easy? Well, this is how we need to be in our interactions with other people—but of course the arena of human interrelationship is a much more difficult arena than athletics. In our relationships with each other, being an armorbearer is being so accomplished in exhibiting the character qualities that matter most that we make it look easy. You should know that making something look easy takes a level of excellence only achieved through intense focus and time. Remember, much of this is caught, not taught. Therefore, it takes time. Be patient. Being human is not so easily done: just look around.

---

## We must be willing to regroup, and then retry our influence and our impact.

---

And look at Joseph's story again. Joseph's father tells the oldest brother, Judah, who is responsible for the success of the mission to get food, that he has failed—in fact, that his decision has brought tragedy on their family. How would you respond if your dad told you that you were the biggest failure possible? You would likely get mad, maybe even to the point of never speaking to him again. You might let holding on to that anger be a "banana" you couldn't let go of for years.

But Judah does not reply with anger or bitterness, even though he had to be wounded in his heart. He regroups! The ability to regroup, to get up after you've been knocked down, is one of the chief qualities of an armorbearer. So many people, once things go bad, are marked by defeated thinking for the rest of their lives. But Judah regroups, and proposes to the father that Benjamin's safe return will be his personal responsibility. He says in verse 9, "if Benjamin does not come back, I will be guilty forever" (in essence, I will not come back). Notice something important here: because Judah was able to regroup, it helped Israel regroup. This is what being an armorbearer is about.

In verse 11, Israel reflects the positive impact of Judah upon his thinking when he launches into a plan to help bring about a good outcome—taking the best fruits, balm, honey, spices, myrrh, almonds, double the money, etc. Then, in verse 14, Israel arrives at the place he never should have departed from, "And may God Almighty give you mercy before the man." He returns to standing on the foundation of trusting God to work things out. He regroups on the foundation of faith in God, and then retries his influence and impact. Israel goes from "you have dealt wickedly with me" to "If I am bereaved, I am bereaved" (a statement of his acceptance of God's will in this matter).

When we leave the ground where we trust in God, we end up in the prison of defeated thinking. And many people find it very hard to let go of defeated thinking. Why? Primarily because of our familiarity with our own personal failings. Defeated thinking is a mental prison whose guards are named "I can't." "I can't" will rob you of your freedom and your power. We must realize that a key ingredient of salvation is freedom: freedom from the tyranny of our sins, freedom from the burden of past mistakes, freedom from the devastation of shattered dreams. Christ called and we answered because we heard Him proclaiming freedom to the captives.

*Why, then, are so many Christians still not completely free?* Why are so many Christians in bondage to negative thoughts, depression, and discouragement—and almost as much as non-Christians? Because we have a cunning enemy and a conniving flesh that immediately set about laying traps for us: traps such as legalism, materialism, and consumerism. These traps are so successful that we soon forget to take hold of our freedom and instead we settle for less, just like the monkey. These traps are designed to get us to settle for less so we will stop moving forward into all that God has waiting for us; we get trapped because we cling too tightly to what we believe instead of what God says. Do not settle for a salvation that does not bring freedom from past sins, freedom from doubts about the future, and freedom from fears about failure. When Jesus proclaimed freedom to the captives, He meant it, and it is up to us to get up and walk out of our prison cells and live free. It is up to us to never be satisfied with anything less than complete freedom in Christ.

Too many of us have stopped short of taking hold of all that our salvation has to offer. We have stopped short of being armor-bearers. There is an anonymous quote that captures well what lies before every servant-leader: "I expect to pass through this world but once; any good thing that I do, let me do it now; for I shall not pass this way again."

Stand up, armorbearer! Your time has come. Rest assured, you are made of the right stuff! Find a warrior hard-pressed on every side and wade into the thick of the fight with him. Declare loudly over the din of battle for all to hear: "Do all that you have in mind. Go ahead; I am with you heart and soul!"

For more information about
Gerald Watford
&

*Armorbearers:*
*The Revolutionary Choices of*
*Servant-Leadership*

please visit:

*revglwj@aol.com*
*https://www.facebook.com/gerald.watford.7*

. . . . . . . . . . . . . . . . . . . . . . . . . . . . . . . . . . . . .

For more information about
AMBASSADOR INTERNATIONAL
please visit:

*www.ambassador-international.com*
*@AmbassadorIntl*
*www.facebook.com/AmbassadorIntl*